Arthur Harrison (the company's first foreman) and Bert Holmes (its first welder).

© Porter Press International

First published 23 October 2020

ISBN 978-1-913089-17-7 (softback)
978-1-907085-97-0 (hardback)

Published by Porter Press International Ltd

Hilltop Farm, Knighton-on-Teme,
Tenbury Wells, WR15 8LY, UK
Tel: +44 (0)1584 781588
sales@porterpress.co.uk
www.porterpress.co.uk

Design and text by Martin Port
Edited by James Page
Printed by Gomer Press Ltd

COPYRIGHT

ACKNOWLEDGEMENTS

Thank you to the following people for their invaluable assistance with producing this book:
Lord Bamford, Nigel Chell and Andrew Frith.

JCB
SCRAPBOOK

Celebrating 75 years of engineering innovation

Martin Port

Porter Press International

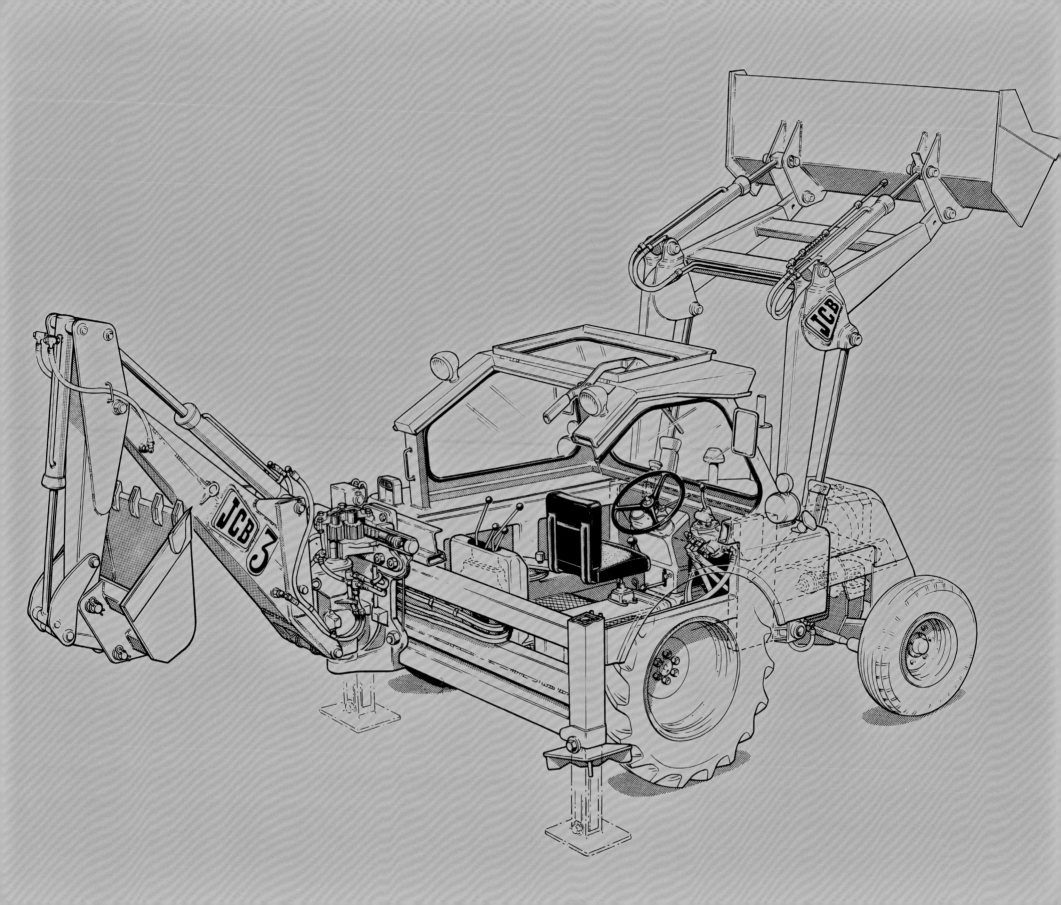

Contents

Foreword

When my father, Joseph Cyril Bamford, started the company in 1945, he did so with a grit, determination and dedication that has, I am pleased to say, remained at the core of JCB.

From the humble rented garage in Uttoxeter grew a business that now reaches all four corners of the world, with 22 factories operating in four continents, yet at the very centre remains our headquarters in Rocester, Staffordshire – ensuring that we retain a Great British pride in everything we do.

On 23 October 2020, we celebrated our 75th birthday, and although this was a milestone moment – one of so many I have been proud to be part of – it also comes in a year that has seen so much challenge, on a personal and business level. Once again though, those three words have come to the fore and the grit, determination and dedication of those at JCB have seen the company respond to the global situation and provide help and support for those that most need it.

This book, I hope, will act as a celebration of the past 75 years: the innovations, the engineering excellence, and the achievements of all those who have made up the wider JCB family from its inception in 1945. I hope, too, that it will serve as inspiration for the next generation – those talented young people currently rising through colleges and universities, including our very own JCB Academy.

Here's to the next 75 years.

Anthony Bamford
October 2020

In the beginning...

With JCB celebrating a major milestone in 2020, we take a look at the history behind the Bamford name and how it gave rise to one of Britain's greatest engineering success stories

Henry Bamford's foray into ironmongery eventually led him to help his eldest son, Samuel, to develop his own manufacturing business.

HENRY BAMFORD & SONS

The engineering origins of what would become JCB arguably began when the Bamford family started out as blacksmiths in Uttoxeter in the 1820s, followed by the opening of an ironmonger's shop by Henry Bamford in 1844. The first of his children, Samuel, was born the following year, and after leaving school he opted to develop some of his own ideas for various products.

This soon resulted in a range of pumps, cheese presses and curd mills for starters, plus a patented design of iron tap that gained a silver medal at the 1864 Staffordshire Agriculture Show. With the cost of having items cast at local foundries being rather expensive, he persuaded his father to buy some land so that he could start his own and soon the product range was widened to include oil cake mills, sheep racks, haymakers and milk carriages, among other items.

Before long, Henry Bamford was helping Samuel expand the growing business and, with his other children all playing their part, they would become extremely successful with a range of tools and machinery designed to improve productivity.

The company, now with considerable manufacturing space in the area, would eventually develop a stationary engine to power some of the various machines they had manufactured, and in time it would be very difficult to find a farm in the country that didn't possess a Bamfords of Uttoxeter product.

A company float adorned with some of the latest machinery during a local carnival in the early 1900s.

Left and above: two images that demonstrate the sheer scale of the Bamford business – stationary engines being assembled on the opposite page and two different types of grinding mills above.

Right: a range of Bamford products now on display in The Story of JCB exhibition at the Rocester headquarters.

JOSEPH CYRIL BAMFORD

Born in 1916, Joseph Cyril Bamford was initially destined to join the ranks of the family business started by his great-grandfather Henry.

After a spell at Stonyhurst College in Clitheroe, he joined one of the largest machine tool manufacturers at the time, Alfred Herbert of Coventry, and in 1941 was called up to serve with the Royal Air Force. He was invalided out in July that year, and shortly after he married in 1942 went to work in the Gold Coast (now Ghana), where he was in charge of several bauxite mines – bauxite being the main component of aluminium and therefore of great importance in the production of aircraft.

After coming back to the UK and working for English Electric, Bamford then returned to the family fold, but after being told by his father's cousin that his services were 'no longer required' he decided, aged 29, to carve out his own future.

On 23 October 1945, JC Bamford Excavators Ltd was founded, and for 30 shillings a week he rented a small garage opposite the local cinema and set about turning some of his ideas into reality. Apart from the rent, his first outlay was a second-hand welding set. With this, and a supply of post-war scrap metal, he began building his first product…

1945 THE FIRST TRAILER

Using steel that had been sourced from now-defunct bomb shelters, and wheels and axles from an Albion truck, Joseph Cyril Bamford constructed his first piece of equipment – a trailer with a screw-type lift to enable it to tip. When it was finished, he attempted to sell it for £90 at the local market, but eventually a deal was struck at just £45.

All was not lost, however, and Bamford took the buyer's old cart in part-exchange. A coat of paint, some coachlines and the JC Bamford signature later, and the cart was sold for another £45.

Joseph Bamford had realised his initial asking price as a result of the combined sales – and offered an insight into his determined approach in the process.

The garage in Uttoxeter where Joseph Bamford began his business. Many years later, a replica would be built at the company's Rocester premises.

Joseph Bamford's second trailer included a hydraulic aspect to its operation and was made completely from steel – the first of its kind because all trailers had previously been constructed from wood. By this point in 1948, the company had moved to nearby Crakemarsh Hall.

Did you know?

In the early 1950s, a finance house noted within their card record system that young Mr JCB 'had little chance of expansion'. How wrong they would be...

Above: spotting an opening in the market, Joseph Bamford began buying surplus ex-US Army Willys Jeeps. He would then convert them and sell them as shooting brakes, and would use one himself to deliver his own products.

Right: on the very same day that Bamford first opened his company doors to the world, son Anthony was born.

Joseph's wife Marjorie and son Anthony watch as Bill Hirst and Arthur Harrison work on a loader bucket. Hirst and Harrison were two of three initial employees who were brought in to cope with early expansion and demand. Hirst was taken on as a tea boy and rose to the rank of director.

The former cheese factory at Rocester that would become JCB's home in 1950.

Did you know?

Joseph Bamford's office was converted from a deep chicken run. Over three inches of droppings had to be cleaned out and the smell lingered for months...

1950 MOVE TO ROCESTER

Joseph Bamford soon found himself working seven days a week – a fact that did not sit comfortably with his landladies at both the garage in Uttoxeter and Crakemarsh Hall. For them, the Sabbath was still designated as a day of rest. As a result, he set about looking for new premises and in 1950 moved the company to a former cheese factory in Rocester – its most recent purpose having been as a cattle and chicken farm.

It was Bill Hirst who initially told Bamford about the potential new site. Living in Rocester, Hirst reckoned that if he could persuade the boss to relocate, he would gain an extra 10 minutes in bed each morning!

Over the ensuing years, the former Wiltshire United Dairies factory was expanded – taking the site from just shy of an acre to 175 acres, with the main development into a then-modern working space being undertaken in the 1960s.

Today it remains the world headquarters of JCB, and although it may be virtually unrecognisable as the site that Joseph Bamford acquired all those years ago, the company's roots have never been forgotten.

Right: Mr JCB with the welding set that he bought for 50 shillings in 1945. The equipment is still owned by the Bamford family and can be found at the Rocester headquarters.

JCB – A BRIEF TIMELINE

1945
Joseph Cyril Bamford began the business that would come to bear his initials.

1945
Anthony born on 23 October – the eldest son of Joseph and Marjorie Bamford.

1946
Joseph Bamford launches his first trailer with screw lift mechanism.

1960
The JCB 4 is launched – the decade would see many new models added to the range.

1961
JCB buys first aeroplane – a de Havilland Dove (Exporter 1), used to bring customers to the UK.

1963
JCB 3C hits the market, beginning a line of backhoe loaders that would evolve over decades.

1980
The versatile 3CX hits the market – a major development of the successful 3C.

1985
The company celebrates another milestone – its 40th birthday.

1986
The 100,000th backhoe loader rolls off the JCB production line.

1998
A second JCB Transmissions factory is opened in Wrexham.

2000
A JCB 3CX is used by raiders in an attempted robbery at the Millennium Dome.

2001
Joseph Cyril Bamford passes away at the age of 84.

2003
JCB India is officially formed, cementing years of success in the country.

1948
The Major Loader, designed to fit a Fordson Major tractor, is introduced.

1950
JCB relocates from Crakemarsh Stables to a former cheese factory in Rocester.

1953
The first backhoe loader hits the market – the JCB Mk1 Excavator.

1968
The company's headquarters at Rocester undergoes massive redevelopment.

1971
Considered by Mr JCB to be one of its most significant machines, the 110 is launched.

1977
The 'Dancing Diggers' display team has its first practice session.

1978
The first components are produced at the new JCB Transmissions factory in Wrexham.

1990
Anthony Bamford becomes Sir Anthony as he receives a knighthood.

1991
JCB's revolutionary new tractor, the Fastrac, is revealed to the world.

1996
Another decade, another record as backhoe loader production reaches 200,000.

2010
The JCB Academy officially opens its doors to the first intake of students.

2013
JCB output reaches the milestone figure of one million machines.

2018
The groundbreaking first fully electric JCB machine is launched.

2020
Prototype hydrogen-powered excavator unveiled.

JCB through the years

Over the past 75 years, JCB has illustrated how a company can grow and evolve, from humble beginnings to a global force in industrial engineering. Here are just some of the highlights...

1948 MAJOR LOADER

Joseph Bamford's 'eureka' moment came with the idea of using his knowledge of aircraft hydraulics to revolutionise the lifting mechanism on one of his first trailers, but the future of what would become JCB was undoubtedly secured with the launch of the Major Loader.

With most loading still done with fork or shovel and a good helping of elbow grease, the hydraulic system built into the Major Loader would prove to be a welcome introduction. Developed as an attachment for the Fordson Major – one of the most popular tractors of the period – it sold for about £150 and was later developed so that it could be fitted to a variety of different tractor models, thus widening its appeal.

Even at this early yet pivotal moment in the company's history, versatility was at the forefront of the design process and the Major Loader shovel could be swapped for the optional muck fork attachment, crane jib or bulldozer blade.

Thousands of Major Loader kits were sold and, with a maximum working height of just under four metres, would help to transform the agricultural landscape of Great Britain and Europe.

MASTER - LOADER *Patents pending*

IT SCRAPES · IT SCOOPS
IT PUSHES · IT PULLS
IT LOADS · IT LIFTS

Manufactured in Great Britain's only factory solely devoted to loader design, development and production

PRICE (Ex works) **£60**

J. C. BAMFORD

LAKESIDE WORKS · ROCESTER · UTTOXETER · STAFFS · ENG

(OUR ONLY ADDRESS · NO CONNECTION WITH ANY OTHER FIRM)

Telephone: ROCESTER 283   Telegrams: "LAKESIDE, ROCESTER"

In 1951, Joseph Bamford followed up the success of the Major Loader with the Master-Loader – a smaller version working on the same principles, but ideally suited to less demanding jobs around the farm such as mucking out. The Master-Loader retailed at £75 and had a production run in the region of 2,000 units.

1951

1952

A mid-mounted mower attachment was launched in 1952 and once again enabled farmers to modify their tractor to good advantage.

Did you know?

Inspiration for the JCB lozenge-shaped logo came from the way that the founder's initials had been painted into the cutter guide for Bamford's mid-mounted mower.

HALF TRACKS

For FERGUSON · FORDSON · NUFFIELD · DAVID BROWN Etc.

1953

It was a visit to Norway in 1953 to market his half-tracks that led Joseph Bamford to a pivotal discovery. Spying a hydraulic backhoe, he immediately bought one and had it shipped back to the UK before drawing inspiration for his next move. Here, a young Anthony Bamford can be seen on one of JCB's half-track conversions.

The Si-draulic Loader was available for most major tractor models, including the Fordson, and was, for many years, the only side-mounted loader available. With a maximum lift of 3.4 metres, it proved to be extremely versatile, as this French-built Hydro Fourche example demonstrates.

Did you know?

The Si-draulic could be detached from the tractor in just 10 minutes. It was also made under licence in France and marketed as the Hydro Fourche.

1953

The Load-Over was the first machine to bear the now-familiar JCB lozenge-shaped logo. As can be seen below, the model retailed for £1,495 and, despite building only a handful of examples, it proved to be an important step in the JCB story and evolution.

From the 1950s onwards, JCB relied upon its attendance at various shows around the UK in order to promote the product range. One new machine for 1953 was the JCB Load-Over – thus named due to the fact that the bucket could be lifted up and over the operator, dumping the contents at the rear.

1953 MK1 EXCAVATOR

Following Joseph Bamford's purchase of a hydraulic backhoe from Norway, he quickly set about working on an improved design, and in 1953 the JCB Mk1 Excavator was born. In essence, this was a Fordson tractor with a hydraulic excavator fitted to the rear, but the turning point was the addition of a Major Loader bucket assembly at the front; Europe's first 'backhoe loader' was officially born.

The Mk1 Excavator was originally available with either a concrete block counterbalance fitted to the front or an air compressor, but with the front bucket in place it officially became referred to as the Mk1 Major Loader.

There was a choice of four buckets plus an optional cab, and while the entire outfit was available as a kit to be fitted by dealers to tractor units, a pre-assembled complete machine could be purchased direct from the factory.

This also carried the first hint of what would later become the well-known colour scheme: while those dealer units would be predominantly red and blue in colour, the factory-supplied machines were yellow with red wheels, loader and excavator assemblies – a theme also employed on the company delivery trucks, as can be seen on the opposite page.

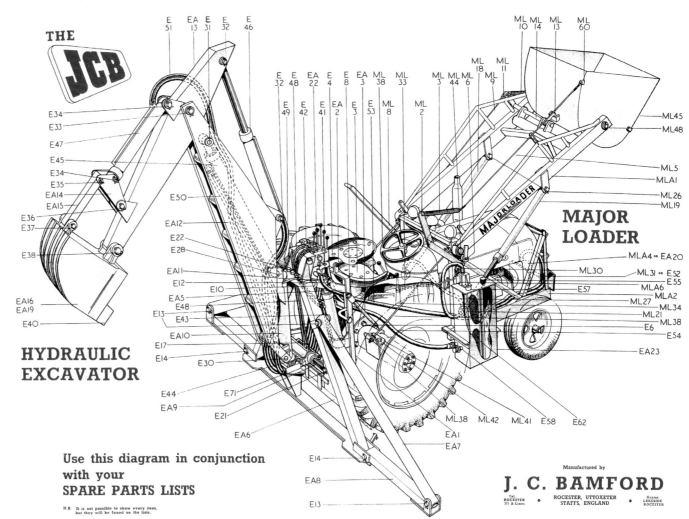

THE JCB

HYDRAULIC EXCAVATOR

MAJOR LOADER

Use this diagram in conjunction with your **SPARE PARTS LISTS**

N.B. It is not possible to show every item, but they will be found on the lists.

Manufactured by

J. C. BAMFORD

Tel. ROCESTER 371 & Lines • ROCESTER, UTTOXETER STAFFS, ENGLAND • Grams LAKESIDE ROCESTER

The Mk1 Excavator can be seen here with both Major Loader (far left) and concrete counterbalance weight (left) fitted to the front of the tractor unit.

Right: a Mk1 Excavator pictured in 1956 aboard the JCB Bedford. The truck's colour scheme would be applied to factory-assembled excavators.

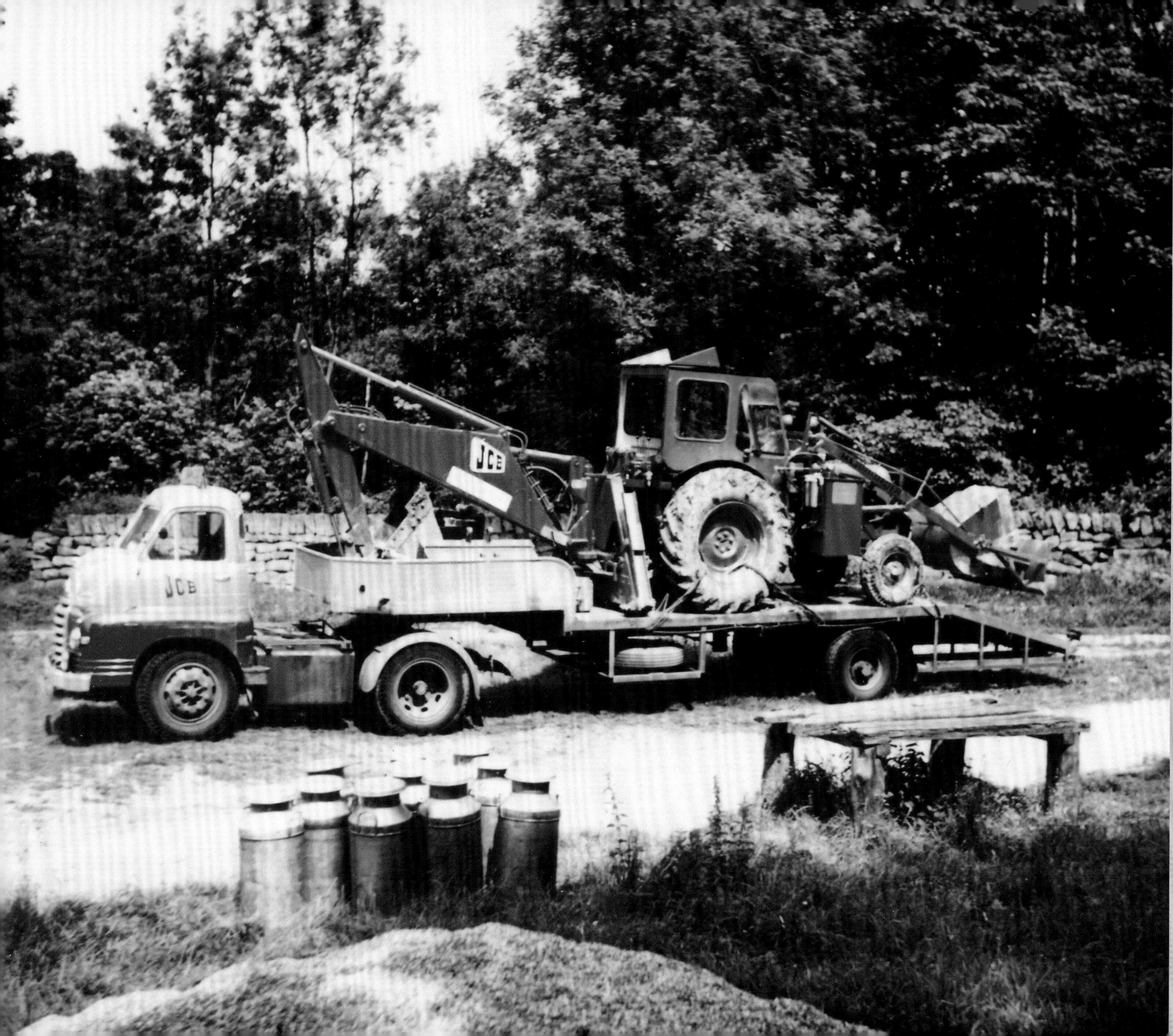
JCB
JCB

WHAT'S IN A NUMBER?

With JCB having quickly become an established brand, Joseph Bamford was keen to apply his moniker where possible – including to the company car fleet. Unfortunately, he had to resort to unusual tactics in order to secure the desired registration numbers, eventually ordering 10 scooters from a Blackburn dealer. The condition of purchase was, of course, that they were issued with the region's prefix. JCB 1 to JCB 10 were subsequently supplied and the numbers eventually transferred to more powerful vehicles!

No. 564955

Certificate of Incorporation

I Hereby Certify, That

ROCESTER SERVICES LIMITED

is this day Incorporated under the Companies Act, 1948, and that the Company is Limited.

Given under my hand at London this   Nineteenth   day of April   One Thousand Nine Hundred and Fifty six.

Registrar of Companies

In April 1956, a new service business was launched – Rocester Services Limited. At the same time, the company officially became JC Bamford (Excavators) Ltd.

1957

The JCB Loadall was a natural evolution of the Major Loader and boasted increased strength for the construction market. In 1958, it was renamed the Loadall 65 and is seen here incorporated into the new Hydra-Digga excavator.

1960 JCB 4

Designed for contracting and civil engineering, the JCB 4 was, to begin with, built around a Fordson Power Major tractor unit. Like the Hydra-Digga/Loadall 65 that came before, the external hydraulic reservoir of old was a thing of the past and the model used its hollow chassis sections to carry the fluid so vital to its operation.

Thanks to the larger hydraulic ram, the JCB 4 had an uprated bucket capacity – just one example of improvements throughout, the 4.8 metre-wide 'A' frame aiding stability, the unique front axle boasting a certified rating of 70 tonnes, and the extended reach of 6.7 metres all proving to be unrivalled specifications at the time.

With a cab large enough to take five people, this new model could be used quite effectively as transport from one construction site to another, but without doubt its unique appeal lay in its combination of power, versatility and refinement for the user – attributes that would become synonymous with the JCB name.

THE NEW JCB 4

REPRINTED FROM THE CONTRACT JOURNAL 19/1/60

Above: the JCB 4 production line in full swing – the Fordson Power Major base eventually giving way to the Super Major skid unit.

Left: the versatility of the JCB 4 is demonstrated here in 1962 – a stunt that would come to inspire the famous JCB 'Dancing Diggers'.

Did you know?

In 1963, excavator operator John Lohan dug up £5,000 while at the controls of his JCB 4. The bounty had been buried in an old tin box in Ancoats, Manchester!

CAT. No. 410

Demonstrations unlimited in your area this week

See the 3 by JCB
you name the day, we will be there.

Above: to satisfy demand from smaller contractors, the JCB 3 was launched in 1961 and helped secure another corner of the increasingly competitive market. The innovative Hydraslide rear assembly enabled the 'kingpost' to be moved across the width of the machine rather than being centrally fixed, as in previous models.

Right: a JCB 3 in action as it makes light work of removing an area of paving outside Webberleys Ltd in the Hanley area of Stoke-on-Trent. Another example of the new model can be seen below, filling a trench outside nearby Milton railway station.

JCB 3C STREET STAR DIGS DEEP FOR NEW POOL

These days, the idea of an 'A-list' celebrity having their own swimming pool would be considered the norm, but in 1963 it was hardly *de rigueur* – even for someone at the height of their profession such as actor Pat Phoenix, better known as Elsie Tanner in *Coronation Street*. Phoenix couldn't resist the opportunity to get behind the controls of a JCB 3C and duly helped with the excavations taking place at the bottom of her garden. Her home and new pool were subsequently featured in the 30 June edition of the *TV Times*. Judging by the broad grin, she enjoyed her latest, yet brief, role as a JCB operator!

The "JCB 3c" is seen here working on the new Sandiacre bypass on the A52 Derby to Nottingham. Overleaf the bridge carries the bypass over the M.1 London to Yorkshire motorway, now in an advanced stage of construction. Contractor for bypass and bridge: M. J. Gleeson Contractors Ltd.

SPECIFY JCB

1963

Above: three JCB 3Cs at work on the Sandiacre bypass in Derbyshire, 1964. The 3C was a more powerful version of the JCB 3 and became the highest-selling backhoe loader in the UK when launched in 1963 at a retail price of just £2,800.

Above: what do two JCB employees drive away from their wedding in? The skip of a company Dumper, of course! Publicity Department secretary Dorothy Warren and Machine Shop drill operator Bob Boot tied the knot in 1964 before being driven to the reception by JCB chauffeur Harry Moult.

Clearly it's not just children who dream of finding a JCB in their stocking at Christmas, as this selection of festive-themed images and illustrations from the JCB magazines *Earthmover* and *Talkback* show!

1964 MR JCB DELIVERS BONUS TO STAFF

Less than 20 years after Joseph Bamford made his first trailer, he delivered a speech to JCB employees from the very bed of that original model. The reason for his address? To announce that, following the previous year's sales figure of £8 million, each member of staff would enjoy a share of a £250,000 bonus.

The speech was made on Friday 3 January, and with employees taking home an extra £40-500 depending on their length of service, it is safe to assume there were many happy employees returning from work that evening! Just one example of why JCB has enjoyed the benefits of such a dedicated and content workforce.

PROFILE Anthony Bamford

Clockwise: a young Anthony with father Joseph Bamford; one of Bamford's proudest achievements is taking JCB into India with an initial deal with Rajan Nanda, chairman of a local tractor manufacturer; three generations sharing a love of engineering.

On 23 October 1945, Joseph Cyril Bamford began the company that would soon bear his initials... on the very same day that son Anthony was born.

With the Bamford family working tirelessly to transform the germ of an idea into a fully fledged and profitable business, Anthony's involvement was often, at first, subconscious as he would be taken by his mother in his carrycot in the family Austin A40 pickup to collect parts. After leaving school at 16, he embarked on an engineering apprenticeship with Massey Ferguson in France before returning to immerse himself in the family business.

In 1972, Anthony Bamford established the first subsidiary of JCB in Paris – an aspect of the company that would serve a network of independent distributors in the country – and three years later, following his father's decision to retire, he became JCB Chairman and Managing Director.

They may have been large and impressive shoes to fill, but Bamford set about moulding an already successful business into one that he would be equally proud to develop and progress into the future, taking on board some key lessons from his father in the process.

"He taught me always to reinvest capital and always to look at the entire world as a potential market. Above all, he taught me to always consider what is really right for the future of the business, even if that means short-term problems."

After four years in charge, Bamford set about opening the company's first factory in India: "I had travelled there as a teenager and loved the place – so exotic, charming people, so many different languages. But there was, and still is, a strong English influence that I also found attractive."

The new working environment wasn't without its challenges, of course – there were restrictions and rationing – but despite the obstacles Bamford was determined that JCB could succeed. The company is now the biggest construction equipment supplier in India, providing him with one of his proudest achievements.

As with his father, Anthony Bamford's dedication and vision saw JCB go from strength to strength, exploring new markets and innovating wherever possible. In 1990, his

'We produce people capable of being proper engineers – and that's what Britain needs'

LORD BAMFORD

continued efforts were rewarded with a knighthood in the Queen's Birthday Honours List, and in 2013 Sir Anthony became a life peer.

Another of his major achievements was the founding of the JCB Academy in 2010, in a bid to reinvigorate Britain's tradition of manufacturing. A total of 800 students, aged 13-19, study engineering-related subjects every day alongside a wider curriculum, with the simple aims of tackling the nation's shortage of engineers as well as putting something back into the local community.

"After the Academy, they come to JCB itself or one of our partners – or they may go on to university," says Bamford. "We produce people capable of being proper engineers – and that's what Britain needs."

Since becoming Chairman, he has taken JCB from a one-factory operation in Staffordshire with a turnover of £43 million to a global business with 22 plants around the world employing more than 12,000 people making more than 300 different products, yet his commitment to the UK is unswerving: "This is our home – rather like Mercedes-Benz is based in Germany, JCB is based in Britain. A strong home base is very important for business."

His interests include gardening and farming, but he also enjoys motorsport and was the inspiration and driving force behind JCB achieving a world land speed record for a diesel-powered car in 2006. The JCB Dieselmax, powered by two JCB engines, reached a speed of 350.092mph on the Bonneville Salt Flats in Utah, a record the company still holds today.

In total, more than 700,000 JCB engines have been made, powering the company's distinctive yellow diggers and loaders in over 150 countries around the world – testament to the strength of leadership JCB has enjoyed.

Above: the newly titled Lord Bamford with wife Carole, daughter Alice, and sons Jo and George with their respective wives, Alex and Leonora.

Left: Lord Bamford shows HRH The Prince of Wales around the new JCB Academy – a unique facility investing in young people and the engineers of the future.

Did you know?

In the early 1960s, a JCB 3C was used to dig a new seal pond at Twycross Zoo. All went well until a friendly chimp called Sam decided to get his hands on the controls!

Right: a JCB 3D gets up close to these giraffes in order to lend a 'helping bucket' at feeding time. There has always been a strong link between JCB and the animal kingdom – as demonstrated by Joseph Bamford (above right). He introduced wildlife to the lakes at the Rocester headquarters and new breeds of wildfowl are added every year.

An updated Mk II range was introduced in October 1968, featuring larger cabs and various refinements to previous 2, 2B, 3 and 3C models. This 3C Mk II was also available in 'high lift' specification for the loading of gritting lorries – a feature clearly not required on this beautiful summer's day at the beach.

Even from the early days of the company, the desire to export and take advantage of potential global markets was evident. These photographs perfectly illustrate that hunger, with an impressive number of new models arriving at the docks in Le Havre, France, in the late 1960s.

Above: the JaCoB cartoon strip appeared in *Earthmover*, an early in-house magazine. In this strip from 1965, JaCoB is given a helping hand from a JCB bucket to take the chequered flag.

Did you know?

JCB has one of the UK's longest-established employee magazines. In existence since 1964, it has a circulation the size of a commercial newspaper!

A JCB 3C II repeats the stunt first attempted in 1962 – this time over the top of the Bamford fleet Datsun 240Z, bearing the registration JCB III.

PROFILE Michael Lee

Photographer Michael Lee owes more than one debt of gratitude to JCB. Not only did the company provide him with a career spanning 54 years but, by his own admission, Joseph Bamford quite possibly saved his life.

The son of a Uttoxeter vet, Lee was employed as the company photographer in 1964 and was put to work documenting everything from JCB's expansion, development of new machines, involvement in motorsport and, of course, photographing key visitors.

Naturally, this included being behind the lens for visits by members of the Royal family, an honour which is not lost on Lee as he recalls his first Royal assignment – photographing Prince Michael of Kent.

"I remember being very nervous," he explains, "but he came up to me and told me to nod before every photo I took and that he would then smile. From then on, I was at ease for evermore and I did that with all the Royals."

That impressive roll call has included Her Majesty The Queen, HRH The Prince of Wales and Princess Diana, but thanks to the Bamford family interest in motorsport, he counts himself equally lucky to have met and photographed

luminaries such as Sir Stirling Moss, John Surtees and James Hunt. "If it wasn't for my coming here I'd never have seen half the things or met half of the people that I have," he reflects.

Although over those 54 years with JCB, Lee's world changed considerably – from going everywhere with his trusty Nikon, Leica and Linhof cameras and several dozen rolls of 35mm film in hand, to the development of digital photography – his feelings about the company remained consistent throughout: "Ask anyone who has worked here for a long time and they will tell you what sets the place apart is that you are treated as a person who matters, you are part of a team and part of a family business with strong family values at its heart."

And what of Mr JCB's life-saving act? One November morning in 1964, Lee was making his way to the Rocester premises when he hit a sheet of ice in his Hillman Imp. The car left the road and rolled several times before coming to a stop; it was "bent like a banana" and Lee had extensive facial injuries.

"I didn't know where I was for a moment, and next thing I knew, Mr Bamford was tearing all of the electrics out of my car to stop it catching alight," he explains. "He then got me out of the car and remained perfectly calm while he called for assistance. Had he not been so quick thinking, who knows what may have happened?"

Michael Lee was company photographer from 1964 until 2018 and was responsible for recording over 50 years of JCB's history.

Celebrity endorsement is almost always a good thing, and in 1965 comedian Ken Dodd jumped aboard a JCB while in Newark to open a new show home on behalf of the National Coal Board. Just minutes before, the machine had been digging footings, but Dodd didn't let that stop him using it as a platform to showcase his talents.

SHEFFIELD
WEDNESDAY
FOOTBALL
CLUB Ltd.
WHITELEY BRIDGE 545/6/7/8
JCB
7
HOBSONS
FRONT
YET
328

JCB A GOOD SPORT

By default, the effectiveness of the JCB model range through the years has positioned it at some of the world's premier sporting venues when construction work has been called for, and when you think about sporting successes during this decade, England's victory in the 1966 World Cup undoubtedly springs to mind.

Before the country could host this spectacle, however, some of the football grounds needed to have a 'makeover' – including Hillsborough, the home of Sheffield Wednesday.

Here (left and below) we have a tracked JCB 7 being put through its paces during the early stages of a revamp of the Leppings Lane end in 1965. Four matches would eventually be played at the stadium during the tournament, but the new model secured its spot in the starting line-up before Sheffield-born Gordon Banks took his place between the posts the following year.

Above: a JCB 3C at Edgbaston Cricket Ground in what appears to be a neatly staged publicity shot near the Stanley Barnes stand.

Right: a day at the races for this JCB – the Royal Berkshire-liveried 3C II carrying out maintenance duties at Ascot Racecourse.

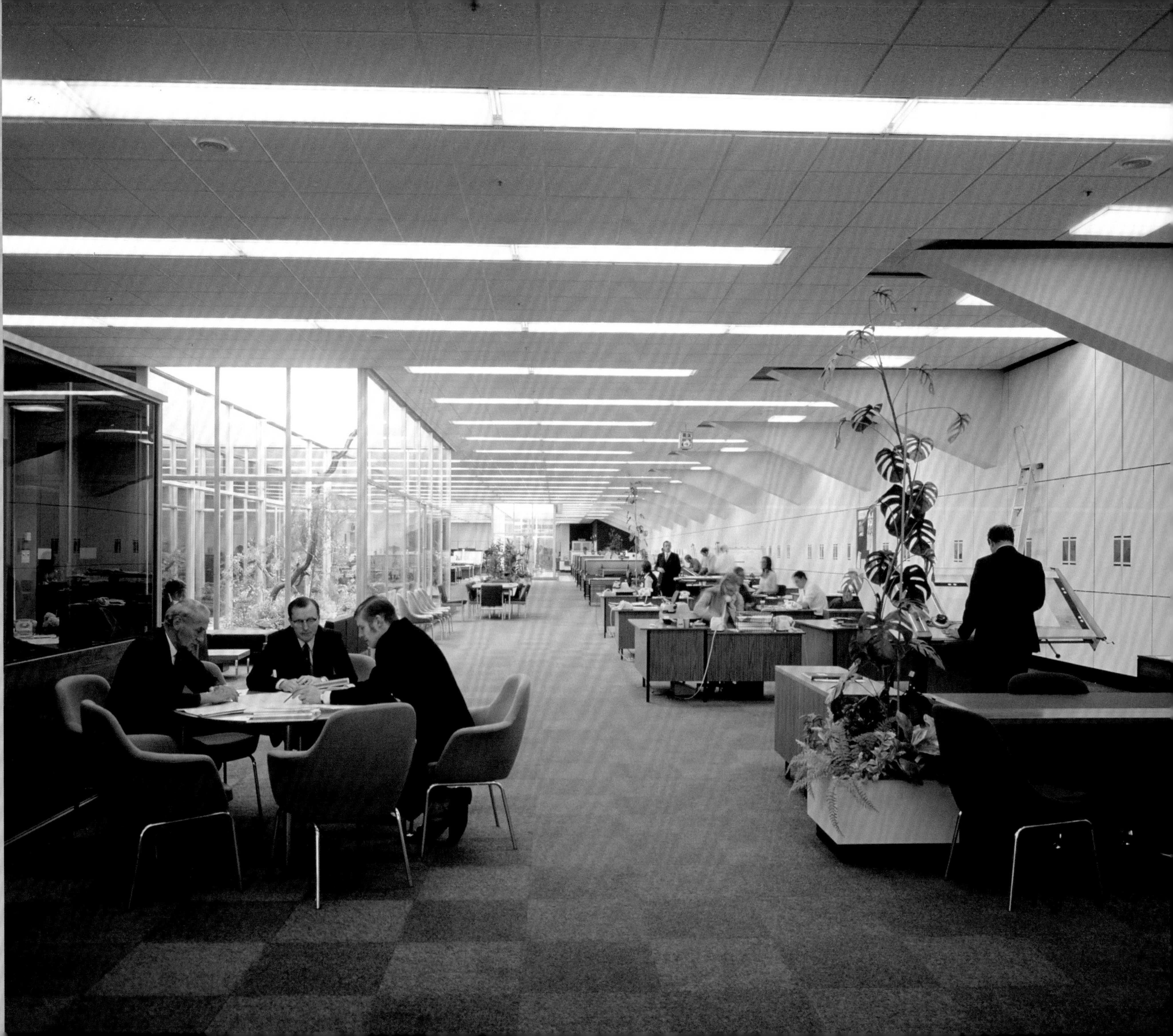

OFFICE LIFE IN THE 1970s

JCB prided itself in being at the forefront of developments in the field, so it should come as no surprise to discover that the Rocester head-quarters were approached in the same innovative manner.

As the 1960s gave way to the 1970s, the company offices kept pace and, as so neatly demonstrated by this set of photographs, could easily be described as cutting-edge at the time – both in terms of the facilities on offer and also thanks to the interior design.

With colourful and bright spaces providing staff with the working environment needed to inspire creativity, the infrastructure behind it was equally important, with a healthcare support system that offered employees easy access to on-site medical practitioners. To this day, the staff at JCB enjoy the benefit of having a doctor, dentist, nurses and physiotherapist within the confines of the Rocester base – another innovation courtesy of the Bamford family.

From the all-important drawing office to the on-site medical facilities (pictured here is Sister Enid Harvey – a key member of the medical centre team), JCB has always led the way by providing employees with the environment they need to perform at the highest standards, although it would be another decade before the computer revolution would herald the next major office revamp.

In 1970, JCB also opened up an office in Baltimore to harness the growing potential in North America.

ARTICULATION

1971 JCB 413

The 413 was the first JCB-designed loader to reach the construction market – previous offerings having been kits available to bolt on to established machinery such as the Major Loader – but with it came another innovation for the company: articulation.

Introduced in 1971, the JCB 413, and subsequently the 418 (1973), featured a new articulated chassis that introduced greater manoeuvrability while ensuring that traction was maintained thanks to the specially designed oscillating centre pivot, which kept all four wheels in contact with the ground.

The cab was mounted forward of the central pivot in order to offer the driver maximum visibility, and the model boasted JCB's automatic 'return to dig' feature that enabled the driver to concentrate on moving the entire unit into place before shovelling the next load.

413 PULLING POWER

Even the mighty JCB 413 proved to be little match for Walter Cornelius when he used his considerable strength to pull the eight-ton machine at Brighton Toy Fair in 1974... with his teeth! Organised by Tonka Toys, the winner of multiple World's Strongest Man titles dragged the JCB 413 25 yards along the promenade, claiming it to be "a good test of strength."

Cornelius fled his native Latvia in the 1940s, rowing across the Baltic Sea with a bullet wound in his stomach, eventually settling in Peterborough and working as a lifeguard at the city's lido. He taught thousands of children to swim and raised a huge amount of money for charity carrying out a wild array of feats. Those included walking on his hands for 153 miles and eating raw sausages, breaking more than 50 world records in the process.

PROFILE
John Wheeldon & Jane Staley

Between them, father and daughter John Wheeldon and Jane Staley devoted almost a century of service to JCB and in doing so were also responsible for one of the most heart-warming images within the company archives: the pair, clad in JCB overalls, chatting while perched atop a backhoe loader in the 1970s.

Wheeldon may well have introduced his daughter to the company, but his involvement began in 1946 when, as a local farm worker, he bought a screw-tipping trailer from Mr JCB. Two years later, he was the sixth person recruited by Joseph Bamford, going on to become the company's first ever demonstration driver and then establishing the JCB Training School – teaching employees

and customers how to operate and maintain JCB's latest models. This even extended to a young Anthony Bamford.

With his trademark handlebar moustache, Wheeldon was a well-respected figure, as remembered by former JCB Inc President Roger Eve: "To me, John, along with Mr Bamford and Bill Hirst, represented the essence of JCB – dedication, ingenuity, customer responsiveness and always looking for a better way. John lived that phrase we all had on our desks – 'Problems are solutions in disguise.'"

Wheeldon's daughter Jane joined the company in 1964, starting her career at JCB as a junior typist at the age of just 15, but, thanks to an admitted combination of hard work and good fortune, progressed to the position of Personal Assistant to Lord Bamford – a post she held until her retirement in 2013, when she stepped down from her full-time role to work part-time.

"It's amazing to think that when I started here at Rocester, this was the only factory in the UK," she remembers. "JCB still holds its family values dear, which for a global company is remarkable."

Left: father and daughter share a 'JCB moment' and (inset) Wheeldon holds Mr JCB aloft on the occasion of 1963's bonus. Below: Jane in the early days of her career and more recently with Lord Bamford.

The bright yellow of a 3C II looking rather incongruous against the New York skyline of the 1970s, yet it illustrates well the global appeal that JCB had developed. Bottom right: back on home turf with some London-based promotion for a chain of department stores.

SOLID ROCK

In March 1970, legendary rockers Status Quo released their latest single *Down the Dustpipe*. Although it didn't feature on the recording, a JCB 3C II helped out with a live performance from Francis Rossi, Rick Parfitt, Alan Lancaster and John Coghlan on ITV's *The Golden Shot*.

Providing a platform for their appearance on Bob Monkhouse's prime-time TV game show, the group perched on various parts of the 3C, with drummer Coghlan atop the JCB's engine lid!

Two sides of the dizzying heights that JCB enjoyed in the 1970s thanks to its hard-earned success: visits from legendary sports broadcaster Dickie Davies (above) and Marjorie Wallace, Miss World 1973 (below).

The JCB 110 was the first loader to use a hydrostatic system and was considered by Joseph Bamford to be one of the company's most significant achievements at the time. The tracked loader would go on to win a Design Council Award in 1972, a year after its launch.

PROFILE The Boot family – 600 years of JCB service!

1974

Bill Boot on his retirement in 1974, having started a trend that would last four generations of his family... so far!

2020

It's a remarkable, unprecedented story of one family's connection to JCB: the Boots of Rocester and Denstone, near the World HQ, started their amazing record of working for JCB when Bill Boot clocked on for the first time in 1949. He eventually retired in 1974, but his lasting legacy is a lot more than just his many years of dedication.

Bill and his wife Lucy – who worked in the canteen – had nine sons and a daughter and all but one went on to work for JCB. Tony, Dereck, Ken, Bob, Bill, Dennis, Les, Ron and Ruby became the second Boot generation to serve the company.

The tradition continues – six of Bill's grandsons now work for JCB, as well as three great-grandsons. As of the 75th anniversary year, the family has notched up a combined 600 years' service to the company over four generations.

Bill's son Bob, who started work in the 1960s and went on to enjoy a career spanning 40 years with JCB, says: "One of the first things my father did was help lay the foundations on the new JCB factory at Rocester. It is a company that has changed so much, but so many things have stayed the same, particularly on the

personal front. It may have factories in all four corners of the world but it is still based on the values that started it up in Staffordshire 75 years ago."

Bill's grandson Gary said his family were very proud of their links to the business. Gary, who started working for JCB in 1986 and retired in 2020, says: "I always wanted to join from an early age. My dad, Dereck, would come home and tell us stories of the company and Mr JCB and that sparked my interest. Mr JCB loved the idea of family connections to his company."

Gary's brothers Andrew and Steven are identical twins and both work for JCB. Andrew says: "I think the way in

> ## 'One of the first things my father did was help lay the foundations on the new JCB factory at Rocester'
> **BOB BOOT**

which it has panned out over the generations has been brilliant. I joined in 1983 on a Youth Training Scheme and haven't looked back from there, and my brother has now been working for the company for about 11 years in total."

Steven adds: "Being identical twins makes it difficult for our colleagues but, to be honest, there are so many Boots I find it difficult to keep up myself!"

The fourth generation is made up of great-grandsons Shaun, Daniel and Leigh Boot. Shaun, who has worked in the Tool Room for 20 years, says: "There is definitely something in the blood of the Boot family that makes us want to work at JCB. Knowing that my dad, my grandad and my great-grandad all worked here really does make me sit back and think. I'm really not sure what our family would have done for a living if it wasn't for JCB!"

The burning question for colleagues and the family alike is, will the fifth generation of Boots walk through the door and join the company?

Shaun says: "I have a six-year-old daughter and my brother Daniel has a six-year-old son. I wouldn't be surprised if they decide to follow in the family tradition."

Launched in the early 1970s, an 808 crawler excavator hard at work in Albina, Suriname where average rainfall can reach 99 inches.

Nothing wrong with a spot of patriotism: from Union Jack waistcoats to a 110 framed by London's famous Tower Bridge – JCB has always been proud of its British heritage.

1977

Despite previous single-machine demonstrations of agility, this was one of the first practice runs for what would become a firm favourite at events – the famous JCB 'Dancing Diggers'.

In 1979, JCB explored the opportunities that existed within the Indian construction market and embarked on a hugely successful joint venture with tractor manufacturer Escorts of India. A new factory would be built in Ballabgarh, near Delhi, and the JCB name would become as well known in India as it was in the UK.

Up, up and away in my beautiful balloon: the multi-coloured promotional hot air balloon, bearing a giant JCB logo, lifts off from the ground in a controlled ascent.

1979

Part of the JCB medical centre team, Sister Enid Harvey and first aider John Henshaw, show off the new Carlton ambulance.

WHAT'S YOUR EMERGENCY?

In 1979 came the introduction of a new ambulance at the JCB site. Bearing the familiar company prefix on the numberplate, the Vauxhall Carlton estate was fitted out to 'county specification', matching that used by ambulance services around the UK.

The specialist conversion cost £1,500 at the time, but even then, of course, that was a small price to pay for the potentially life-saving treatment and quick response offered by the new vehicle.

In the corresponding issue of *Talkback*, the company magazine, JCB's medical officer at the time, Dr Roger Brookfield, used the vehicle's announcement as an opportunity to stress the importance of keeping factory roadways clear of obstructions in order to keep response times down.

1980 3CX & SITEMASTER

At the beginning of the new decade came the launch of what could be considered one of JCB's most important machines – the 3CX.

Its predecessor, the 3C Mk III, was outselling the competition by a massive margin, yet the forward-thinking board – now headed by Anthony Bamford following his father's retirement in 1975 – was certainly not going to be complacent. An ambitious programme of development, referred to as 'Project 200', was embarked upon.

The result was the 3CX, an all-new model, and while that was a success, JCB responded to customer feedback with the 3CX Sitemaster just a year later. With a six-in-one clamshovel with flip-over forks and an extending dipper with crane hook, this was the versatile machine it needed, and as a result it became one of the company's most successful offerings.

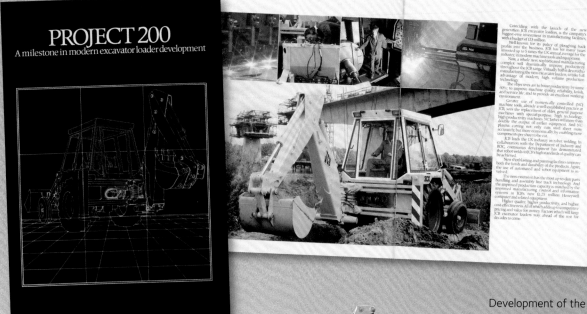

Development of the 3CX was done under the codename 'Project 200' and was the result of years of research and development work.

PROFILE Dr Roger Brookfield

Innovation at JCB covers far more than just the development of its new machines and associated technologies – something that can be perfectly demonstrated by a look back at one of the company's key employees: Dr Roger Brookfield.

Previously a General Practitioner in Cheadle, Staffordshire, Dr Brookfield joined JCB in February 1974 at a time when very few companies had any form of workplace medical care. With just over 1,000 employees in place at the time, he recognised the importance of such a system and duly played a major part in developing the occupational health strategy at the Rocester headquarters.

Over the next four decades, Dr Brookfield offered care

Above and far right: Dr Roger Brookfield pictured during the 1970s in the early days of his JCB tenure, with Enid Harvey assisting, and (right) at the end of his career as he retired.

and support to countless other employees – both as a medical practitioner and as a friend, although one story, recounted by Brookfield in 2011, clearly demonstrates the lengths he was prepared to go to as part of his role: "Having learned of my knowledge of anaesthetics, Mr JCB asked me to perform a minor operation on one of his diseased Koi Carp. I removed part of the fin and put the carp back into his pond, but the rejuvenated fish swam away before Mr JCB could inspect my work, leaving him splashing around in the water looking for the fish!"

Dr Brookfield retired in 2011 and sadly passed away five years later, but his legacy – a comprehensive on-site medical facility that is available to all employees and which is named in his honour – is testament to his hard work while at JCB.

Did you know?

Sculptor Walenty Pytel developed 'The Fosser' with the help of scale models before handing over to JCB's Experimental Department and Works Engineers.

1980 'THE FOSSER' SCULPTURE ERECTED

Standing 40ft high and measuring 41ft across, 'The Fosser' was created by sculptor Walenty Pytel at the request of Anthony Bamford. The name is a rough translation from the Latin for 'the digger' and at the time was the largest metal sculpture in Europe.

Weighing 36 tonnes and with foundations extending 20ft into the Staffordshire ground, the creation was developed by Pytel, who admitted that the abstract was a challenge and a departure from his usual subject matter of animals and birds.

Designed to withstand high winds, the sculpture is based around a central 808 model turret ring with bracing struts, and includes four 807 crawler boom and dipper assemblies, three loading shovel buckets and eight 3C excavator ends.

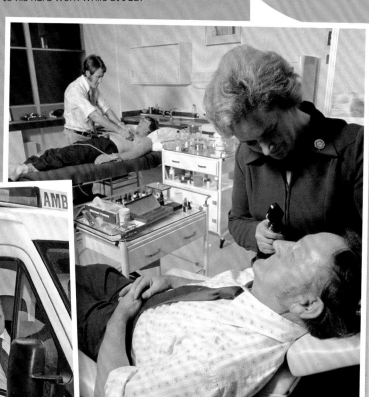

In the early 1980s, JCB Sales purchased a 33ft American-built Travel Cruiser. The V8-powered converted mobile home was used as a sales and conference centre at exhibitions throughout Europe. It could seat 14 and included a fridge and state-of-the-art microwave oven.

1982

In true 'high tech' 1980s style, the launch of the 807C was not presented by a familiar face from the world of television, but was instead headed up by Argon, a radio-controlled robot. The pair emerged from a cloud of dry ice!

The ultimate show of affection? You can't get much bigger than painting a mural on the side of your house in order to demonstrate your love for a brand!

1984 530 LOADALL

JCB launched its first 'telehandler' – the 520 – in 1977, and over the next few years it underwent a natural evolution incorporating a series of improvements. In 1984, the 530-4 was launched. By that time, its most recent predecessors had gained four-wheel drive and this new machine was no different. The combination of improved traction and interchangeable attachments made it a versatile choice for the construction and farming industries alike.

MILITARY SPECIFICATION
JCB 410M-IB
ROUGH TERRAIN FORK LIFT TRUCK

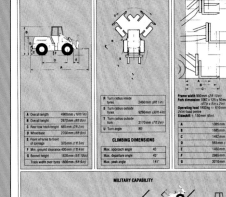

THE JCB RANGE OF
COMBAT SUPPORT EQUIPMENT
MILITARY SPECIFICATION

All JCB machines are extremely versatile and robust, have numerous build options and are available with a wide range of fitments.

JCB is the largest entirely British-owned manufacturer and exporter of earthmoving machines, with vast experience of hydraulic systems, proven in all climates and conditions.

JCB machines are produced under strict quality control, using high technology equipment, in one of Europe's most advanced factories.

Currently, JCB exports some 60% of production to 113 countries, with a service and parts back-up commitment of over 400 JCB Sales and Service centres worldwide.

Uniquely, immediate parts availability from the JCB factory in England is never less than 99%, and despatch can be effected within 24 hours.

MORE FOR YOUR MONEY. EVERYTIME.

410M-IB SPECIFICATION

1984 410M-1C

The JCB 410M-1C was unveiled as a military-specification version of the standard 410 and was in direct response to an unprecedented order of more than 700 machines by the British Army. Apart from the obvious colour change, the 410M-1C was modified to allow for use in a wide range of conditions – one being the lower cab height, originally devised for an earlier order from the Royal Air Force and allowing the unit to be transported by air.

Swapping in a different gearbox provided a higher road speed for the wheeled loader, while other changes included a different wiring setup, headlamp protection, special lighting arrangements and personal storage space.

Below: West Country-based distributor Holt JCB Ltd opted to give two of its Bedford CF350 vans a striking makeover in the early 1980s. The parts sales vans were customised with large-scale graphics of the then-current 3CX machines and could be seen throughout Devon and Cornwall.

"A BIT MORE TO THE RIGHT... HIGHER... AH, THAT'S LOVELY!"

1986 BACKHOE LOADER MILESTONE REACHED

While the previous year was cause for celebration as the company hit 40, 1986 saw the 100,000th backhoe loader roll off the production line to resounding cheers.

In the bucket were Anthony Bamford and Chief Executive Gilbert Johnston, and it reflected JCB's continued position at the top of the tree in the backhoe market.

The special-edition 3CX Sitemaster was subsequently raffled to raise funds for the Lighthouse Club Benevolent Fund, which lends support to those affected by accidents on construction sites. The total raised was £72,000 – the winner being contractor Sir Robert McAlpine, who immediately handed the machine back to the club so that it could continue to boost its funds.

Did you know?

The term 'JCB' entered the Collins English Dictionary in 1987: 'A type of construction machine with a hydraulically operated shovel on the front and an excavator arm on the back.'

The JCB 930 was just one of the new additions to the range in the mid-1980s. It had a lifting height of five and a half metres with a capacity of 2,600kg, making it a valuable tool to have at your disposal.

PUBLIC (HOUSE) DISPLAY OF AFFECTION

Derbyshire fans of the JCB name will no doubt have fond memories of an aptly named pub in the village of Buckland Hollow. When Jim Balls decided in the early 1980s that he would branch out from his job at the helm of local plant hire company JC Balls & Sons, he became the owner of the Grade II-listed pub and christened it The Excavator.

With 20 JCB machines to the company's name, Balls decided to add one more: a 1963 JCB 1 backhoe loader, which, after a brief period out on hire, he promptly refurbished and perched on top of the pub's roof!

With appropriate memorabilia inside, The Excavator became something of a mecca for backhoe fans, but although the name remains today, the digger has been replaced by a JCB Mini CX and relocated to the safe confines of the beer garden.

PROFILE
John Moult

Design Engineer John Moult joined JCB in 1961 and was immediately involved in the development of its latest model, the 3C – including its innovative 'swing carriage' system, which allowed the backhoe arm to slide across the width of the excavator.

"Mr JCB came up with the idea," recalls Moult, "and it was our job to make it work. He was constantly looking to improve and make machines perform even better."

Those improvements sometimes took things 'down to the wire', as Moult remembers: "We were helping with last-minute changes to a prototype due to be exhibited at Crystal Palace. We ended up working through the night, but at 12am Mr JCB disappeared... returning with some bread and bacon before making sandwiches to keep us going! You always knew that your hard work was appreciated – that's one of the best things about working for JCB."

In 1999, Moult went to work in JCB's India plant, running the design engineering department, and after his retirement in 2002 returned there while on holiday. "The difference was unbelievable," he smiles. "JCB has always been amazing at investing and it was impressive to see just how much it had grown. It is so satisfying to know that I played a small part in that."

Staffs earthmoving 'giants' pass a 40-year milestone

IT WOULD be all too easy to dismiss Anthony Bamford as the local lad who made good without really trying too hard.

Eight years ago he was handed the reins of the family's multi million pound firm — JCB.

By Sally Maitland

At the same time he vowed to resist the temptation of becoming a mere figurehead of what is an internationally renowned business.

His 3,900 employees in Staffordshire know him as "the working chairman." His elegantly furnished office at the company's Rocester headquarters has three complete glass walls which means employees can see him at work and he can see them. He is seen surveying the open plan set-up from outside the office.

His huge, elaborately carved desk is piled with reports and, of course, the phones never stop ringing.

Charming

And if more proof were needed of his hectic schedule, it took me nearly a month to find a free afternoon to fix an interview.

It was worth the wait — he is an extremely charming man, quick to...

The rock, in the company's well-known red and yellow stripes, will be dished out to employees' youngsters this weekend at JCB's 40th anniversary celebrations — but more of those later.

The spectacular success of the company, who are now ranked number two in the world with their earthmoving machines, is the classic rags to riches story.

Anthony's father, Joseph Cyril, formed JC Bamford Ltd. in a tiny garage at Uttoxeter, when he was 29 with 30 shillings and a second hand welding set.

Annual turnover this year is expected to top a record £150 million. JCB now hold a significant 17 per cent share of the market and are market leaders in 55 countries as well as the UK.

But the firm, who have received six Queen's Awards to Industry and been granted a Royal Warrant, have never moved from their site in the tiny Staffordshire moorlands village.

Competition

He spends at least one day a week in Europe and is a regular visitor to the firm's plants in America, Canada, India as well as France.

Apprenticeship

he was 20 "as a lad on the shop floor" but not at his father's insistence.

"He was relatively indifferent when I said I wanted to learn how JCB have managed to survive — and thrive.

"By keeping it fairly simple," said Mr. Bamford. "Most of the people are based here, apart from the...

which has hit many of the construction equipment businesses, it is intriguing to learn how JCB have managed to survive — and thrive.

1985

Just one of no doubt hundreds of articles that have appeared in the press during the company's history – this one, from Stoke's *Evening Sentinel*, talks to Anthony Bamford about the company's history, ethos and reaching the 40-year mark.

JCB ON POLE POSITION WITH RACING LEGENDS

What do motor racing legend Sir Stirling Moss and TV presenter Clive James have in common? Apart from both being pictured with one of JCB's model range, the pair took to the track when Moss took the non-driving Antipodean and tutored him in preparation for a celebrity saloon car race before the 1988 Australian Grand Prix.

From one motor-racing legend to another, and in 1986 Nigel Mansell made a flying visit to JCB's Rocester factory. Taking the opportunity to swap his Williams Formula One car for a JCB Sitemaster, he gladly signed autographs and posed for photographs throughout his tour.

Naturally, JCB wished him luck: at the time, Mansell was leading the World Championship, but a blown tyre with just 19 laps to go during the Australian Grand Prix led to McLaren's Alain Prost clinching the title instead. It would be another six years before Mansell would finally wear the crown in 1992.

1980s VISITORS OF NOTE

Throughout the decade, JCB and the Bamford family welcomed a considerable number of notable visitors to their Rocester premises.

The company's position as one of the UK's leaders of industry has never gone unnoticed, and as the previous decade drew to a close, JCB would regularly open its doors to Prime Ministers and members of the Royal family.

Recently ousted PM James Callaghan visited in 1980 and would, some years later, be followed over the threshold by Margaret Thatcher, who drove a backhoe off the production line under the watchful eye of Anthony Bamford, before signing the boom arm of one of the company's latest models. She later admitted to him that she didn't drive!

The Duke of Edinburgh 'popped in' in 1981 and Prince Michael of Kent was shown around the JCB 3CX 4, proudly displaying the Royal Warrant crest, while in 1989 HRH The Princess Royal officially opened the new Rocester showroom. Another highlight undoubtedly came in July 1988 when HRH The Princess of Wales visited the company's stand at The Royal Show, establishing a family connection that would later be continued by HRH Prince William.

Clockwise from above: the Duke of Edinburgh, the Princess of Wales, James Callaghan, Prince Michael of Kent, Margaret Thatcher, and HRH The Princess Royal – just some of the members of the Royal Family and government that have visited.

1988 712 & FARM MASTER

Another two new models saw the light of day in 1988 – the 712 and the Farm Master, although each had very different target markets.

The 712 was an articulated dump truck unit with a low and wide body, and all-wheel drive as standard – ideal for shifting dirt loads around site.

In contrast, the 406 Farm Master was pitched at those looking for a replacement for the old farm tractor, although one of its major selling points was shared with the 712 because they both boasted an articulated chassis that contributed to the Farm Master's impressive manoeuvrability.

The 406 Farm Master offered the agricultural market a pleasant and effective upgrade to old tractor units, and boasted an impressive inside turning radius of just 1,810mm.

A BRIGHT FUTURE

A very productive decade for JCB drew to a close with a special exhibition at the Design Council. Intended to champion the basic ethos of good design that the company had become famous for, JCB Industrial Designer Chris Hampson and David Woodhouse, a student from Coventry Polytechnic, came up with some visuals that hinted how the JCB model range might look in the 21st century.

The exhibition was a first for the Design Council – it didn't normally examine the work of a single company, but recognised the outstanding contribution made by JCB.

1990 2CX

With the JCB 3CX performing so well, it was only a matter of time before it spawned an off-spring: the 2CX. Produced in reaction to industry requests for something smaller, the 2CX allowed for the specific task of carrying out highway repairs without the need to close more than the lane that was being worked on, thanks to its diminutive dimensions.

Knighthood for JCB chief

1990

Right: the JCB logo has appeared on various vehicles over the years, but this 530hp Chevrolet-engined sprint car was certainly something different! Racing in the Pro Sprint Circuit of California, Steve Bettencourt's vehicle was sponsored by Ortons Equipment Co Inc – a JCB dealer in Stratford, CA.

A KNIGHT'S WELCOME INTO A NEW DECADE

The 1990 Birthday Honours List resulted in a special moment for Anthony Bamford – he was awarded a knighthood in recognition of his contribution to British industry. Sir Anthony passed on his thanks to the staff by rewarding them all with a day off to be taken on Friday 22 June.

In 1990, Sir Anthony Bamford was also presented with a Midlands business award for individual leadership following an exceptional period of success and continued reinvestment.

Boss of export boost company wins top award

Staffordshire industrialist Anthony Bamford today won a top Midlands business award for individual leadership.

Mr Bamford took over as chairman of earthmoving equipment maker JCB in 1975 on the retirement of his father, Joseph Bamford, the firm's founder.

Since then the company, based at Rocester, near Uttoxeter, has seen its sales soar from £43 million to £377 million in 1988 – the seventh successive year of record sales.

Profits have continually been ploughed back into the business and £80 million has been invested in new plant in the past eight years.

JCB is now 20th in the league table of Britain's engineering exporters.

Anthony Bamford

Last year Mr Bamford received one of France's top honours, Chevalier de l'Ordre National du Merite, for his services in working towards the single European market in 1992.

At the awards ceremony in Birmingham, Mr Bamford said: "Ours is a practical earthy business and simple ground rules have brought about our success.

"Success lies in recognising our customers as kings who deserve excellence in their dealings with JCB."

Birmingham-based Brittanic Assurance won the marketing award for its recent launch of a new personal pension plan.

Plasplugs of Burton-on-Trent carried off the award for enterprise with a new range of tiling products.

Leicester-based Gent Ltd won the product development award for its new fire detection and alarm systems.

The judging panel was headed by Sir Eric Pountain, chairman of Tarmac, Wolverhampton.

It took precision and skill when a JS150W was balanced on top of eight Wedgwood bone china cups for a record attempt in 1996. The 15.5-tonne machine was delicately placed by senior Wedgwood engineer John Howard. With experts on hand to authenticate the attempt, the record for the greatest amount of weight ever balanced on china cups was duly awarded and recorded for an episode of *Record Breakers* presented by Cheryl Baker.

1991 FASTRAC

One of JCB's most innovative products was released to the global market in 1991: the Fastrac – a genuine high-speed tractor.

With research showing that many agricultural machines spent a considerable amount of time travelling between farming locations, JCB decided to invest £12 million in the development of a suitable alternative to other traditional offerings.

Featuring full suspension, the initial Fastrac models were powered by either a 125hp normally aspirated or 145hp turbocharged Perkins diesel engine with all four wheels being driven through 18 forward and six reverse gears.

This combination enabled the Fastrac to travel at speeds of up to 45mph while hauling a 14-tonne payload – a unique statistic that introduced new levels of efficiency to the modern farming industry.

Launched at the Royal Show at Stoneleigh in 1991, the new Fastrac impressed many, including the Prince of Wales, who acknowledged the need for such a vehicle when being presented with the opportunity to experience the spectacular machine for himself.

DRIVING IS BELIEVING

The JCB Fastrac picked up several awards, including winning the general category for new equipment incorporating innovative ideas at Stoneleigh's Royal Agricultural Show.

FASTRAC 145 Turbo

Did you know?

In 2007, 'The Stig' drove a Fastrac 8250 around the *Top Gear* Dunsfold track, posting an impressive time of just 2 minutes 57 seconds!

1992

Above: time for a spot of 1990s television nostalgia now – in 1992, the BBC show *Challenge Anneka* received help from JCB and Alfred McAlpine with plans to excavate a 13th Century moat before turning it into a facility for disabled anglers in Shropshire.

Below: *Game for a Laugh* and *Beadle's About* host Jeremy Beadle realised a lifelong ambition by enjoying a tour of the Rocester HQ before taking the controls of a JCB excavator.

JCB 185 ROBOT

THE ULTIMATE IN SAFETY AND PRODUCTIVITY

Unique skid steer safety is now available for the widest variety of applications thanks to the new JCB 165 Robot.

This powerful 850kg operating capacity machine has the productive ability and strength to tackle the toughest of jobs in the toughest of environments. With more than sufficient power generated by the high performance 36.5kW (75hp) engine, it proves to be the ideal skid steer to work in demolition, on asphalt top cutting or on numerous demanding bulk handling tasks.

Naturally, it shares all the attributes found in the rest of the Robot range in that it works to the highest safety standards, is easy to

operate, supremely comfortable, allows simple maintenance and is very environmentally friendly.

The fact is, with excellent lift capacities and superb manoeuvrability generating cycle times that are remarkably fast, there isn't a safer bet for the toughest of jobs.

- The unique single loader arm design allows unprecedented levels of safety. It enables the operator to gain safe access to the cab while still providing an exceptional loadover height and loading performance.

- To help maintain excellent productivity, dual hydraulics allow simultaneous operation of various machine functions.

- Servo-assisted controls on the JCB 185 Robot is very easy to use. The operator works the loader while operates machine difficult low lever effort requires tongue is minimised.

- Servo-assisted joysticks most accurate and machine handling.

- Unbeatable manoeuvrability. A low overall height 185 Robot works superb in confined of spaces.

- Substantial ground clearance gives excellent use over the worst terrain.

GENERAL SPECIFICATION

STATIC DIMENSIONS

MACHINE RATING

Rated Operating Capacity (SAE)	850kg
Tipping Load	1700kg

ENGINE

4-cylinder, 4-stroke, diesel engine, direct injection.
Naturally aspirated 3.9 litres displacement. Water cooled.

Gross power @ 2200rpm	
BS AU 141 (a)	56.5kW (76hp)
Nett power @ 2200rpm	
EEC 80/1269	52.5kW (70hp)
Gross torque @ 1200rpm	
BS AU 141 (a)	288Nm (213lbf ft)
Nett torque @ 1200rpm	
EEC 80/1269	283.5Nm (209lbf ft)

Engine service intervals 500 hours.

WEIGHT

SAE Operating Weight
Fully operational with Quickhitch, standard aboard, full fuel tank. Fully glazed cab. 3240kg (7,200lb)

TRANSMISSION

Full servo-controlled twin speed hydrostatic transmission giving 6.0km/h for both forward and reverse in 1st speed and 0-17km/h for forward in 2nd speed.

CONTROLS

Hydraulic over hydraulic servos reduce lever efforts to a minimum.
Twin joystick controls mounted on the resistant are well positioned for easy use. Pilot pattern control is logical and easy to operate.
Joystick mounted auxiliary control push buttons for straightforward control of attachments.
Transmission switch for 2nd speed located at the base of loader servo control.

CAPACITIES

Hydraulic System (inc. tank) – 65 litres (14.44 gal)	
Fuel tank 99 litres (22 gal)	
Chain cases 12 litres (2.67 gal)	
Engine coolant 15 litres (3.33 gal)	
Engine oil 10.75 litres (2.36 gal)	

TYRES

Standard	12 x 16.5 HD 2000
Optional	12 x 16.5 Trac Loader 12 x 16.5 Airboss 7.56 x 15 Busine 252

Solid tyres also available.

BRAKES

The JCB hydrostatic transmission control provides the primary braking service. For parking, the JCB fail safe braking system features oil-immersed, multi-disc brakes for long life and fade-free braking. Operation is spring-on, hydraulically pressure off, activated through either the electrical parking brake switch or the restraint mechanism.

HYDRAULICS

In addition to the main hydrostatic drive pumps, there is a dedicated loader and attachment supply pump. Both the main transmission pump and the loader controls are servo-operated, for ease of use and precise control.

Pump flow: 78 litres/minute at 2200rpm engine speed.

Main relief pressure 220 bar (3200psi).

- Low lever efforts give excellent and easy control of transmission loader and attachments.

- Loader joystick incorporates push button control of attachments.

- Hydraulic supply pipes run neatly along the loader arm for long life and protection against damage.

- Full flow, spin-on type hydraulic oil filter.

- Engine oil throughout for ease of servicing.

- The optional hi-flow circuit provides 140 litres/min pump flow to the base of the machine for operation of high capacity attachments such as cold planers and trenchers.

1993 165/185 ROBOT

Hot on the heels of the Fastrac came another JCB revolution with the launch of the 165 Robot. The new skid-steer featured a single arm loader – much like that used on the company's first bolt-on products in the 1950s – but it enabled the operator to enter the cab from the side instead of having to clamber over potentially dangerous attachments at the front.

At 6.5ft tall and a little over 11ft long, the compact machine still had a tipping load of 1,700kg and was ideally suited to use in restricted spaces within farming and construction environments.

1995 A ROYAL REVIEW

Half a century had passed since Mr JCB started his company and so it seemed apt that in 1995 Her Majesty The Queen visited Rocester and officially opened a replica of the Uttoxeter garage where it had all begun in 1945.

Both Her Majesty and HRH the Duke of Edinburgh toured various parts of the factory and offices before the unveiling, pausing to chat with both current and retired employees, many of whom had dedicated years of service to the company.

Left: JCB enthusiasts could even now go 'off piste' with a selection of excavator-themed knitwear!

Right: another major milestone for the JCB company as employees and Sir Anthony Bamford celebrate production of the 200,000th backhoe loader. More than 23,000 machines would be built in 1996 – testament to the growth in facilities and workforce.

1996

1997

The diversity of the JCB product range is superbly demonstrated here in this shot from 1997. Machines on offer ranged from the 185 Robot to Fastrac and JS160 tracked excavator – clearly something for everyone...

Above: West Ham and England legend Trevor Brooking paid the JCB sales team a visit in 1998, and clearly impressed them with his ball skills.

1997 FORK HANDLES

In a bid to capture a corner of the forklift market worth £6 billion and dominated at the time by German and Japanese manufacturers, JCB unveiled its new Teletruk model in 1997.

As opposed to a traditional vertical-lift machine, the Teletruk hoisted loads using a telescopic boom – a feature that would undoubtedly provide the operator with increased versatility thanks to the extending reach.

PROFILE John Mitchell

Like so many who have spent a considerable number of years at JCB, John Mitchell has been involved with a huge variety of projects, with several different job titles to his name as well!

Mitchell joined the company in 1977. His primary role was Press Officer, and because JCB was soon to reveal the Loadall, it was a case of being thrown straight into the deep end with the launch of one of the most important new machines of the time.

Six years later, and with the UK having been hit by a recession, it became obvious that the continued success of JCB meant capitalising on the potential that existed around the world. Mitchell found himself with a new responsibility – Export Market Development.

He quickly identified the issue: with market support being so heavily weighted to the UK, the global sales teams in far-flung territories were struggling with the fact that much of the material featured UK farmland, rolling fields and obviously British urban and rural backdrops. The result? Some potential customers were struggling to be convinced that the JCB machine, pictured carving its way effortlessly through soft British soil, could cut

it in the most demanding of environments in South Africa, Australia or South America.

Mitchell's solution? Simple: photograph and film the machines proving that they could cope with local terrain by putting them in those very environments. Not only did that give rise to a series of stunning adverts (see page 108), but with the advent of affordable videotape recording, they could actually film the machines in action – as well as the customer's reaction!

Although Mitchell retired in 2014, he has recently been involved in the curation of decades worth of JCB videotape and cinefilm recordings – using state-of-the-art machinery to digitise the footage, correctly identify and label each film and preserve it for the next generation.

This is no exercise in nostalgia, however, as Mitchell is keen to point out. "JCB has always been a forward-thinking company," he explains. "Chances are, Lord Bamford will watch an old piece of footage and spot an idea that he can develop for the future!"

Former JCB Press Officer John Mitchell realised that far-flung markets needed to see machines operating and coping with their local conditions.

One model to be constructed at a new Earthmovers factory in Cheadle, Staffordshire was the JCB 411B – an articulated wheeled loading shovel.

MISTY MOUNTAIN HOP

As the decade drew to a close, a 4CX was shipped in individual bits to help with a very special project.

In order to assist with the building of much-needed flood defences in a remote area of Nepal, a 1997 machine was shipped out to a customer in Kathmandu, but with poor weather and no access by road, the 4CX first needed to be dismantled into manageable sections by Jason Callear, Team Leader in the Backhoe Loader Division, and then airlifted to a location 16,000ft up in the Himalayas.

Callear then had to reassemble the machine – a task that took four days during which he lost 2½ stone in weight and experienced acute altitude sickness. With the JCB then performing its intended task by digging channels that would help prevent glacial waters from engulfing mountain villages, the mammoth effort was definitely deemed worth it.

Left: a second JCB Transmissions factory was officially opened in Wrexham in 1998 by the Duke of Edinburgh, watched by Chief Executive John Patterson. Prince Philip then fired up the machines that would begin the process of manufacturing new JCB axles.

1999 JS330LC

The JS330LC was one of a number of tracked excavators offered by JCB as the 1990s gave way to the new millennium. The LC stood for Long Carriage and provided extra stability compared to the NLC (Narrow Long Carriage), which allowed for easier transportation.

With a maximum dig depth of over eight metres and an operating weight of over 32 tonnes, the JS330 was a formidable machine, perfectly suited to quarrying, demolition and large-scale construction projects.

2000 714, 718 & 722

The Articulated Dump Truck (ADT) range of machines provided operators with several options, including the 714, 718 and 722 – each offering different size and weights suitable for different environments and applications.

The 714 was the lightest with a load capacity of 14.5 tonnes – ideal for sites where potential ground damage needed to be kept to a minimum. The 718 and 722 boasted increased figures for heavier applications – the 722 being the most powerful with a 6.7-litre engine producing 730lb ft of torque and a 22-tonne load capacity.

All models in the range featured dual-circuit brake discs on all four wheels (six in the case of the 722) and the improved Smoothshift ZF transmission setup.

Above: former Bond girl and *Avengers* actress Honor Blackman found herself sipping champagne from the driving seat of a JCB 8015. Fortunately she wasn't at the controls – JCB Demonstration Driver Dave Jeffries used the mini excavator to pour Veuve Clicquot into waiting glasses at a celebrity boules match in London's Covent Garden.

OPEN DAY TREATS

JCB's tradition of holding open days continued in 2000 – this time in order to maintain its charitable support for the NSPCC.

An appearance from TV personality and entertainer Christopher Biggins – a long-term supporter of JCB's fundraising efforts – went down very well, as did an appearance from the world-famous Red Arrows.

The Royal Air Force Aerobatic Team treated visitors to a fly-past over the Rocester headquarters, also taking time to pose for a photo opportunity with JCB Chief Executive John Patterson. Other attractions included JCB strongman Tom Smith and a motorcycle stunt rider jumping through rings of fire – never a dull moment at JCB!

2000 DOME RAIDER

One of the biggest talking points of the year 2000 was undoubtedly the Millennium Dome. Built to celebrate the dawning of a new millennium, it was constructed to initially house a major exhibition but the project failed to attract the anticipated visitor numbers.

As the exhibition neared the end of its year-long tenure, however, the Dome hit the headlines again – this time for a daring 'smash and grab' attempt that saw raiders use a JCB 3CX to force their way through the perimeter fence and into the Dome. Their aim? To make off with a £350 million collection of diamonds on display.

Their plan was foiled by undercover police. They had been following the gang's actions and lay in wait… after having first switched the gems for fakes!

With the failed attempt making the front pages of newspapers around the world, JCB seized the opportunity and ran a series of suitably tongue-in-cheek press advertisements under the headline: 'At last, something in the Dome that's worth seeing.'

Below: following the attempted raid, JCB teamed up with *The Mirror*, offering readers the chance to win a £20,000 De Beers diamond – the prize eventually being delivered by JCB Demonstration Driver John Barnes.

Did you know?

The backhoe loader used in the attempted robbery sold at auction for £10,200 in 2006 – more than twice the anticipated amount!

The Mirror man wins gem

JCB Demo Driver John Barnes delivers the £20,000 three carat heart shaped diamond to lucky winner David Littlemore and fiancée Frances Gladman.

JCB teamed up with The Mirror to offer lucky readers the chance to win a £20,000 De Beers diamond in the wake of the Dome robbery bid.

The promotional idea gave the company two days of extensive coverage in a newspaper which sells 2.2 million copies daily - and proved the old adage that diamonds are a girl's best friend.

For the prize of the De Beers gem was won by Credit Manager David Littlemore, 36 - who immediately decided to bring forward his marriage to fiancée of two years Frances Gladman, 39, by selling the giant sparkler. To win, David correctly answered that Diamonds are Forever was a James Bond film.

The happy news came as Demo Driver John Barnes delivered the gem - supplied by Alexanders The Jewellers Ltd, of

Farnham, Surrey - aboard a 3CX to David's workplace at Marantz Hi-fi, in Longford, Middlesex.

David, of Feltham, Middlesex, said: "When I got the call to say I had won the diamond it came as a complete surprise because I had totally forgotten I had entered the competition.

"We will probably sell the prize because I would be too nervous to keep it at home. Frances and I have talked about marriage but when we worked out the cost we decided to put it on hold and it may be the money we get from the diamond could be used for that."

Although a dazzler, David's prize, a 3 carat pearshaped diamond, was not quite on the scale of the 203 carat De Beers Millennium Star diamond raiders attempted to snatch from the Dome.

Sparkler of an idea

COMPETITORS and machine owners thought the JCB ad campaign pictured left, which was hastily drawn up when the raiders and jewels were safely in custody, was a huge success.

Tony Bennett, of Liebherr Great Britain Ltd, said the newspaper ads were "absolutely brilliant," while one backhoe owner copied the ads and placed them proudly in his cab as he was so impressed with JCB's proactive approach to making the most of the marketing opportunity.

The grand opening of JCB's US manufacturing plant in Savannah, Georgia took place in 2001. Although the new facility had already started producing backhoe loaders the previous year, the official opening was carried out by Lord Bamford and Georgia Governor Roy E Barnes.

2001 CRUISING TO SUCCESS

Another first for JCB as it gathered representatives from every single JCB dealer worldwide for a global sales conference... aboard a cruise ship!

With hundreds of employees on board, this was the company's largest ever international conference, with the cruise liner *Westerdam* eventually docking in the US for the opening of the new Savannah manufacturing plant (left).

Left: Barry Moss ended his 20-year JCB-operating career in style following a £7.5 million lottery win in 2001. The story was picked up by the Rocester company, which helicoptered Moss and his partner Pat to JCB HQ for a factory tour. There was also one last drive of a digger so that he could bury his work overalls.

1916–2001
Joseph Cyril Bamford

One of the saddest days in the company's history came in March 2001, as Joseph Bamford CBE, Mr JCB, passed away aged 84.

With flags flown at half-mast at the Rocester headquarters as a mark of respect, family, friends and staff were left to come to terms with the loss of the man whose entrepreneurial approach and unique insight had built one of the world's foremost engineering companies.

Tributes rolled in from around the world and obituaries paid homage to the man who was, as the *Financial Times* put it, 'blessed with a rare combination of engineering genius and marketing flair.'

The Daily Telegraph told of how he never drank or smoked and would work from 9am to 11:30pm. "The trouble with competitors," he once observed, "is they get out of bed too late and go home from work too early." It was a sentiment that demonstrated a dedicated approach that provided the foundations for success.

'It is with great sadness that I have to tell you that my father, Mr JCB, sadly passed away peacefully this morning, March 1st, at 1:05am'

SIR ANTHONY BAMFORD

The loss of Joseph Bamford was felt throughout the engineering world as well as at the Rocester firm he had worked so hard to build up, and tributes abounded from many significant figures for the family man who created a unique empire.

WHAT THEY SAID...

'To lose a parent is a most sorrowful experience, especially one who by his own efforts has added so much distinction to the family name and to the reputation of our country'

THE RIGHT HONOURABLE BARONESS THATCHER

'He worked incredibly hard and was one of Britain's great entrepreneurs'

TONY BLAIR

'He certainly was someone who has distinguished himself with his creativity and business judgement. I know you and your family will miss him greatly, but as you say – the industry suffers as well'

GLEN BARTON, CHAIRMAN AND CEO CATERPILLAR

'He was always the person who kept us on our toes in terms of engine technology and design and has made a significant and valuable contribution to our business. He is irreplaceable and the world of construction machinery will be poorer for his passing'

MICHAEL J BAUNTON, MD PERKINS

2002 SMALL IS BEAUTIFUL

For years, the desire to have the might of a JCB on site was at the forefront of many a contractor's mind, but sometimes space simply didn't allow for such a machine. JCB first addressed this in the 1980s, and in 2002 the company launched a new range of mini and micro excavators.

These diminutive machines were ideal for smaller sites or for working in confined spaces – as perfectly demonstrated by various publicity and brochure photographs that pictured the mini and micro models such as the 8008 and 8060 displaying their versatility.

The 8008 Micro in particular was designed so that it could fit through a doorway opening, making it perfect for working within an existing building or for access to gardens, where a larger machine would struggle to get on site.

With an 11.5-litre fuel tank, operators could also do an entire day's work without the need to stop and fill up – important considerations when working within restricted environments.

The 8060 Mini was just one of a smaller, yet still powerful, range of machines launched by JCB.

2003

2003 A PASSAGE TO INDIA FOR JCB

Although JCB had enjoyed success in India thanks to a commercial relationship with a local manufacturer, 2003 saw the formation of JCB India Ltd after assuming full control of operations.

The facility near Delhi would go on to experience greater success and JCB would eventually become India's largest construction equipment manufacturer, supplying 50% of all machines sold.

With India proving to be JCB's biggest market every year since 2007, the decision to invest looks to have been another very wise one!

Right: just two years after the death of Mr JCB, his wife Marjorie Bamford also passed away. Aged 85, she had been crucial in helping to found and develop JCB and was described by son Anthony as "the driving force" behind the business.

JCB TALKBACK
SPRING 2004

MRS MARJORIE BAMFORD
1918-2003

MRS MARJORIE BAMFORD PICTURED WITH THE LATE JOSEPH CYRIL BAMFORD IN DECEMBER 1995, WHEN HM THE QUEEN VISITED JCB TO MARK THE COMPANY'S GOLDEN JUBILEE

The statement to JCB's worldwide workforce from Sir Anthony and Mark Bamford

"It is with great sadness that we have to tell you that our mother, Mrs Marjorie Bamford, sadly passed away in the early hours of Christmas Morning. Our mother founded JCB with our late father in October 1945 and she played an immensely important role in the early days of the Company. Her contribution was huge and ensured JCB prospered and grew into the international force it is today. We are all going to miss her tremendously."

FULL TRIBUTE INSIDE — SEE CENTRE PAGES

The JCB 722 was part of the Articulated Dump Truck (ADT) range of heavy equipment along with the four-wheeled 718. The 722 featured six-wheel drive and was powered by a 260hp turbocharged six-cylinder engine coupled to a transmission that boasted six forward and three reverse gears.

2004 500,000th MACHINE

JCB reached the half-million mark this year, with its 500,000th machine exiting the manufacturing plant. The 3CX backhoe loader rolled off the production line in Rocester having had its axles and transmission systems made at JCB's Wrexham factory, and was indicative of the company's growth over the previous decade.

"JCB production doubles approximately every 10 years," explained Sir Anthony Bamford, "so we are eagerly looking forward to the day when we manufacture our one-millionth machine."

Above: paying a visit to JCB in 2004 is Hollywood superstar Joan Collins, who was appearing on stage at the nearby Regent Theatre in Stoke-on-Trent in a production of comedy *Full Circle*. The *Dynasty* star, along with husband Percy Gibson and other members of the show's cast, were given a tour of the manufacturing facilities at the JCB headquarters.

PROFILE Jim Edwards

Above: Jim Edwards with Joseph Bamford, pictured during a visit to the Escorts JCB factory in Ballabgarh, India.

Jim Edwards began his career at JCB in 1965, joining as a newly qualified draughtsman with a weekly wage of £18, although his first experience of the company came courtesy of a college visit while studying for his Higher National Certificate. "Mr Bamford was doing a costing exercise," he recalled. "Every part of a machine was laid out in pieces in the factory and each had a price ticket on it."

Three years later, he found himself working with some very knowledgeable people: Design Director Alec Kelly, Chief Designer Derek Prime, Chief Draughtsman Cliff Ashwell and, of course, Mr JCB himself.

The first project Edwards worked on was the JCB 3C, but it didn't take long before his career developed – first to designer and then Chief Project Manager in the early 1970s. Then, in 1979, he oversaw production of one of JCB's most radical redesigns, the 3CX.

Edwards' career continued in its ascendency, but it was arguably a visit to India – which would go on to see a joint venture established with the Escorts Group and the subsequent

manufacture of backhoe loaders in Ballabgarh – that provided him with some of his most memorable experiences, and in 1983 he returned to the UK to head up the new operation as Technical Manager.

Shortly after, he was tasked with setting up a new Special Products Division. Despite modest beginnings, the design team, with Edwards as Director and General Manager, was fast-prototyping models of what would become the new 2CX – sticks, string and cardboard being used to build small loading shovels.

His experience in India came back to the fore when his involvement in more global development saw the start of manufacturing in Brazil and an increased stake in the Escorts arm of the business in Ballabgarh. Upon his retirement in 2003, after 38 years of service, he offered his thanks to JCB: "I am one of the luckiest engineers in the world... the company is full of opportunities and I have to give Anthony Bamford great credit because he allows you to do jobs which would not be allowed in any other company."

Edwards pictured as part of celebrations surrounding JCB's 65th anniversary in 2010.

2004 FIRST JCB ENGINE

Although it had long been an ambition of the company to build its own engine, it took until the late 1990s before the economies of scale were at a point where this could be considered. Following an extensive period of development, the JCB444 unit first appeared in the 3CX and 4CX backhoe loaders.

Replacing the Perkins engines that had previously been fitted, the all-new 4.4-litre diesel unit was specifically designed for 'off-highway' machines. Built at JCB's Power Systems plant in Derbyshire, the engine boasted four valves per cylinder as well as an advanced common-rail injection system, and proved to be the quietest of its type in production.

The power unit's success was quantified by the fact that by 2017, JCB celebrated the production of half a million engines – enough to stretch from London to Paris – and with a dedicated workforce that had grown from 64 to almost 400!

JCB has never been a company to sit back, and by that point production had already started of a new, fuel-efficient 3-litre engine – the third engine line to be launched since 2004 and building on the success of the JCB EcoMax, with its low-emission combustion system that picked up a Queen's Award for Innovation in 2016.

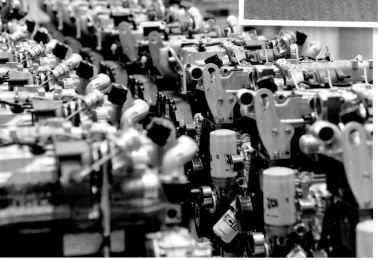

Far left: Mr JCB with a prototype of the first JCB engine in 2000 – a unit that has seen significant development over the past 20 years, resulting in several engine lines capable of providing the impressive reliability and efficiency expected to be found in the latest machines.

2006 GROUNDCARE

The JCB Groundcare division was first established in 2004, but in 2006 came the launch of a full range of products aimed at the lucrative grounds maintenance market – including commercial estates and sporting facilities.

Under the directorship of Jo Bamford, a number of new models were revealed, including several compact tractors, a micro excavator, mini backhoe loader and the Groundhog utility vehicle.

The Groundhog, with its six wheels and compact design, could easily be altered thanks to a range of optional fitments and modified to satisfy specific uses – equally as useful as a game cart, at a golf course or for transporting football equipment at the training ground.

Stoke City striker James Beallie gives a thumbs-up to the JCB Groundhog at the club's Clayton Wood training ground.

2005 JCB CELEBRATES 60 YEARS IN BUSINESS

Six decades had passed since Joseph Bamford had produced his first trailer and as Sir Anthony Bamford cut into a special cake to celebrate the JCB name turning 60, he reflected on how far the company had come.

"I'm extremely proud of what has been achieved," he told reporters, "but we haven't finished the job yet. There is still enormous potential for this company." It is this ambition, previously displayed by his father, that saw the company go from strength to strength – from a garage in Uttoxeter with a handful of employees to a global market-leader with 6,000 staff around the world.

With record profits announced in 2005 of £103 million, it would take only a year to beat that figure: in 2006, JCB would reach £110 million and boost its market share from 8.6% to 9.6% with sales of £1.42 billion – up 23% year-on-year. It sounds like a slice of birthday cake was richly deserved!

2007

JCB picked up a trio of Queen's Awards in recognition of export achievements in 2007. The Loadall Division (Rocester), JCB Compact Products (Cheadle) and International Transmissions (Wrexham) were each handed the award, taking the total Queen's Awards won by JCB over the years to an impressive 21.

In 2007, JCB purchased Vibromax, a German company specialising in compaction equipment, and in doing so extended its model range to include machines such as this single-cylinder road roller.

RESTORING A JCB Julian Carder

Julian Carder, Product Manager for the Backhoe Loader, Hydradig and Site Dumpers, has taken his lifelong love for JCB to the next level. What began as a childhood fascination with the backhoe loader has, over the years, developed not just into a very successful career, but also into an unequalled passion for restoring some of the company's most iconic models.

"I bought my first backhoe loader when I was just 16," he explains. "I then bought a parts catalogue and used colouring pencils to shade in the route of the hydraulic system so I could figure out how it all worked."

That initial act of investigation set Carder off on a path of discovery. Wherever possible, every school project had been directed back to his obsession with JCB, and this theme would continue through a City & Guilds qualification in Plant Mechanics, BTEC National Diploma in Design and Manufacture, BEng Hons in Mechanical Engineering and a BSc Hons in Engineering Manufacturing. It's little wonder that he set his sights on a career at the Rocester firm, joining in 2004.

In 2013, Carder put his considerable experience to use and bought a JCB 3C Mk III with the specific aim of carrying out a full restoration. Why that model? "It was the machine I remembered seeing around while I was growing up. Plus, of course, it's a backhoe loader!"

Although it was in good working order, the eBay listing also caught his attention thanks to the unusual specification, which included the rare semi-automatic option plus a handheld rock breaker – part of an additional 'highway pack' – and soon he was preparing to embark on his first restoration project.

Unsurprisingly, Carder believes in doing a job properly and the 3C took him in the region of 1,500 hours to restore. "Doing something properly and paying attention to getting the details right takes time," he admits. "You can't cut corners, even though it can be challenging."

"So many people jump right in and strip a project down

before taking the time to understand it properly," he continues. "The project then stalls because they can't find parts, forget how something goes together, or baulk at the costs involved. It's much better to assess the machine, list what you need and start sourcing components and working out if you have the necessary skills... or can outsource if needed."

Sourcing parts can be one of the most challenging aspects of any restoration – particularly with older models such as the Mk I Major Loader also restored by Carder, but he admits that his position at JCB has certain benefits: "The company does still stock some parts for obsolete machines, but not many. Although I had to make some myself, I was also able to source some New Old Stock components through our dealer network and have hunted parts down from all over the world."

Another bonus came in the form of JCB's impressive retention of information, which provided Carder with access to original drawings and technical documents – even being able to view the artwork for decals – but the physical side of restoring a JCB should not be underestimated either: "They may have been designed to work for a living, but by the time they are candidates for restoration, they are approaching the end of their original life expectancy. The stress and fatigue visible in the machines from a life of hard labour is considerable and needs to be addressed."

Amazingly, Carder has now restored in the region of 20 machines – from the Major Loader to the 520 Loadall – and admits that the end result is what keeps him putting his restoration talents to good use.

"Bringing something back to life – something that was on the brink of being disposed of – is the most satisfying bit," he explains. "Knowing that I've rebuilt the parts – hydraulic rams, pumps, valve blocks, mechanical linkages – and then seeing it all work as it did when it first left the JCB factory still gives me a good feeling."

Julian Carder's JCB 3C Mk III was running when bought, but was in need of a full restoration. After about 1,500 hours of work, the finished machine was put through its paces – proving it was fit for site once again.

2009 VISIT FROM A PRINCE

Continuing the long line of royal visitors to the Staffordshire headquarters was Prince William. The year also saw the 750,000th machine produced by the company, so it seemed only fitting that the Prince took his rightful place behind the controls and saw for himself how it worked.

Judging by the huge smile, he thoroughly enjoyed the experience and after a tour of the factory, he stopped to talk to the employees and meet some of the hundreds of local schoolchildren that had gathered at the Rocester base.

Sir Anthony Bamford told the Prince: "We have been privileged over the years to welcome so many members of your family to JCB. We have come a long way over the last 63 years, from my father's first product, a farm trailer, to 750,000 machines." He summed up by simply saying: "We would not have done it without our people, the people I call the JCB family."

2010 JCB ACADEMY OPENS FOR BUSINESS

In 2010, another long-harboured ambition was realised – that of an educational facility dedicated to producing the engineers and business leaders of the future: The JCB Academy. Housed in the former Tutbury Mill in Rocester, the Academy was officially opened in 2011 by their Royal Highnesses The Prince of Wales and The Duchess of Cornwall.

The school has capacity for 800 students from the surrounding area and is fitted with more than £1 million of cutting-edge equipment to aid those attending with their studies. Engineering projects are set in association with a number of key partners including Rolls-Royce, Toyota, Network Rail and Bentley, and run alongside GCSE studies in Maths, English, Science and German.

The facility was the first school of its kind in the UK, and 99% of its initial intake of pupils gained A-C grades. In the decade since its opening, it has been over-subscribed every single year.

After the sterling work done by its first Principal, Jim Wade, his successor, Jenny McGuirk, was appointed in 2020 and acknowledged the incredible contribution that the school had made in its first 10 years.

The JCB Academy's first intake of students celebrate their GCSE results.

A pair of JCB Eco backhoe loaders, decked out in Union Jack livery, helped raised more than £70,000 for Help for Heroes, the charity that supports servicemen and women wounded in conflict. One of the new machines toured famous landmarks in the UK's capital to celebrate the company's 65th anniversary, while the second was auctioned, with proceeds going to the charity.

2010 HMEE ORDER BOOST

In 2010, JCB secured a multi-million-pound order from the Swedish Defence Materiel Administration for its High Mobility Engineering Excavators (HMEE).

The model was originally launched in 2007 and was manufactured at the new Savannah plant in the US, gaining significant orders from the US and British Army – some of which ended up in active service in Afghanistan.

The unique machine combines features from both backhoe loader and JCB's Fastrac, resulting in a loader that can travel at speeds of up to 55mph, satisfying the key requirement that it needed to travel at military convoy speed without the need to first load it onto a low-loader truck and trailer.

The four-wheel-drive, 12-tonne HMEE is powered by a 5.9-litre diesel engine, can lift more than two tonnes, and has a maximum digging depth of nearly four metres.

2011 JCB EXPERIENCE OPENED TO THE PUBLIC

A brand-new visitor experience was opened in 2011 at the JCB worldwide headquarters – The Story of JCB.

Occupying 2,500m² of floorspace, the exhibition covers the history of JCB – from early Bamford products such as an 1860 cheese press and No.2 saw bench, through the first hydraulic lift trailer designed by Joseph Bamford, to the Dieselmax-powered land speed record car of 2006 (see page 119).

With breathtaking exhibits for JCB fans, such as a 3C Mk III in 'Dancing Digger' pose and a unique full-size wireframe sculpture of a JS200 excavator, it is little wonder that The Story of JCB received a gold award in the exhibition category at the Roses Creative Awards.

When a pair of elephants fell into a water tank in West Bengal, a trio of JCB 3CX backhoe loaders came to the rescue. The machines pulled the calf out using a special harness before demolishing a section of wall to enable the mother to escape.

2012 LONG ARM USED IN BOMBER EXCAVATION

The long reach of the JCB JS360 excavator was called upon in order to assist the hunt for a missing Lancaster bomber shot down on D-Day in 1944 near Normandy.

The machine, one of several JCBs involved, helped a team of archaeologists excavate the crash site, finding many personal effects and parts of the bomber in the process.

The following year, a JCB was also on hand to support a mission to unearth dozens of Supermarine Spitfires that were rumoured to have been buried in Burma, but nothing has yet been found and it looks as if the rumour was exactly that. The search continues, however...

After JCB produced its 500,000th machine in 2004, less than 10 years had passed before it announced the rollout of its one-millionth unit – an amazing milestone marked by emblazoning a graphic wrap over the glass frontage of world HQ, covering 900 square metres.

In 2012, JCB was honoured with a Queen's Award to mark the success of its backhoe loader – at the time, it was the 27th such award to have been collected by the company since 1969. JCB also celebrated retaining its crown as the world's number one manufacturer of the machine and toasted the achievement and Queen's Award in appropriate style!

Did you know?

If all of the one million machines made by JCB were laid out end-to-end, they would stretch all the way from the UK to Australia!

2014

Plans were unveiled in 2014 for a new JCB facility – a £30 million golf course near the company's headquarters. Apart from helping to boost sales and awareness of the brand, the golf course would also increase the number of jobs in the area – something it has successfully done since its completion in 2019.

MUD, GLORIOUS MUD

The annual JCB Mud Run began in 2012, and its purpose was to raise money for the NSPCC and its Staffordshire service centre, which was itself set up as a result of JCB's charitable fundraising efforts. The Mud Run, which ran until 2017, resulted in a £300,000 boost to the cause and entry numbers swelled from an initial 500 to a record-breaking 3,000, including Lord Bamford's son George (left). JCB's links with the NSPCC were established by Lady Bamford in 1986.

PROFILE Françoise Rausch OBE

JCB has always been known for providing employees with the opportunity to rise through the ranks – something that Françoise Rausch OBE demonstrates perfectly.

Having joined the newly formed JCB France in 1972 as a fresh-faced assistant, she took just nine years to become Managing Director of the subsidiary – a position she held for the next 15 years, having been part of a passionate team that secured a groundbreaking 1,000-machine deal in Algeria that opened up new markets for the company and remains one of the biggest orders in JCB's history.

"When I started at JCB France, we were a very small team of just 12 people and there was no distribution network for our machines, so we set about developing one and the company grew from there."

From 2001 until 2006, Rausch was appointed Head of JCB Sales – a period of time that saw amazing growth. By the end of her tenure, machine sales had virtually doubled to nearly 56,000 units a year.

In 2007, she became Executive Director of JCB Sales and President of JCB Europe and was, as ever, keen to continue the company's growth within the European market alongside expansion in China, India and South America.

In 2013 she was presented with an Honorary OBE for services to industry at a special ceremony held at the British Embassy in Paris, although just a year earlier, Rausch had been awarded France's highest civil honour – the Chevalier de la Légion d'Honneur, marking her 40 years in the construction industry.

"My mother Helene, who is now 96, said on hearing the news: 'Yes that's very good, but don't let it give you a big head!'" she remembers. "So, my feet have remained firmly on the ground."

Françoise retired in 2018 but looks back on over 40 years with the company with nothing but fondness: "Hard work, passion for our great machines and a sense of belonging to the JCB family were part of the formula in France in 1972... and they remain so in JCB people all over the world to this day."

When JCB France moved from Gonesse to Sarcelles in April 1975, Françoise Rausch (right) and Carole Bamford (left) cycled the 10km distance between Paris sites.

2016 HYDRADIG

A number of key features made the JCB Hydradig yet another appealing and innovative machine from the JCB stable. For starters, increased visibility meant that the operator could see all four wheels, which aided manoeuvrability.

With the engine and fuel tank mounted on the chassis, stability was unparalleled and there was a minimal tailswing – an impressive combination that meant that this new wheeled machine could easily outperform rivals, and all in a relatively compact package.

2016 70TH ANNIVERSARY 3CX MK III

As JCB celebrated its 70th anniversary, the firm prepared to launch a Platinum Edition of the 3C Mk III backhoe loader – a model limited to just 70 examples.

It came in a distinctive yellow, red and white livery that offered a nod back to the first 3C backhoes produced by the company. Unlike those early models, however, the Platinum Edition featured air-conditioning, a heated seat and six-speed Autoshift transmission. Each also came with a scale model, retro overalls, polo shirt and a tool bag.

Twelve years after production of the diesel engine began at JCB Power Systems, the team celebrated the half-million mark as the 500,000th unit came off the manufacturing line – enough to stretch from London to Paris if laid out end-to-end!

On Tuesday 21 June 2016, a one and a quarter-scale bronze bust was unveiled at JCB's Rocester headquarters, marking the centenary of Joseph Cyril Bamford's birth. Present at the ceremony were his sons Mark Bamford (left) and Lord Bamford (centre), plus his grandson Jo Bamford (right). The bust is the work of Staffordshire sculptor Andrew Edwards and took five months to create.

2018

As the centenary of the First World War Armistice approached, JCB decided to auction a rather special 16C-1 mini digger in order to raise money for The Royal British Legion. The digger, decked out in unique commemorative poppy livery, was given a final shine by (left to right) Compact Products Assembly Line Operatives John Watson, Andy Minor, Sean Bowers and Mick Capper. It was clearly worth the extra elbow grease – the auction raised £25,500, with the machine being bought by Arnold Plant Hire Limited, a long-time JCB customer.

For many years, JCB has been a company with a penchant for speed, and in 2017 came the announcement of a partnership with Williams Martini Racing. The deal would see JCB branding appear on both the Williams FW40 F1 car and on the race suits and helmets of drivers Felipe Massa and Lance Stroll (right).

2018 TRIBUTE TO JCB'S WWI HEROES

In November 2018, JCB paid tribute to 50 of its employees' relatives – 21 of whom died in The Great War – with the unveiling of a roll of honour and a specially commissioned art installation to mark the 100th anniversary of the Armistice. Designed and made by JCB graduates, it featured 255 porcelain poppies – one for each Uttoxeter, Rocester and Denstone person who lost their lives in the conflict. The poppies were handmade by more than 30 JCB employees – each a former member of the Armed Forces.

2018 X SERIES

The JCB 220X was part of a new range of super-strength machines launched in 2018. The ethos behind the X Series was simple: to develop the strongest possible excavator in order to meet the highest demands on site and in the field.

The 220X was the first model in the series and was the combination of four years of extreme endurance testing, which included 'shaker rig' testing in order to replicate 15,000 hours of tracking and vibration.

Did you know?

The JCB 220X was put through its paces in temperatures ranging from -30°C to 55°C as part of its hot- and cold-climate testing around the world.

2018 ELECTRIC

There is no denying that JCB has always been at the forefront of innovation and 2018 saw the company release another first: the electric mini excavator – a model that addressed customer requests for a zero-emissions machine.

The 1.9-tonne excavator doesn't require any special power source, either – simply plug into a 230v domestic electricity supply and once charged it will happily perform for a full working day on site.

Lord Bamford summed up the motivation behind the 19C-1: "Machines are operating more closely to people as well as digging underground, indoors, near hospitals and in food-production environments. As a result, there is a new zero-emissions sector emerging."

Don't for one moment think that the power source compromises it at all – the machine has the same capability as its diesel counterpart!

Britain's Prime Minister, Boris Johnson, makes an impact at JCB Cab Systems in Uttoxeter. While on the campaign trail in the run-up to the General Election, Johnson took to the controls of a JCB 3CX in order to deliver his message.

Above: JCB continued its involvement in F1 with the announcement of a partnership with the SportPesa Racing Point team. The arrangement would see JCB branding appear on the cars of drivers Lance Stroll and Sergio Perez, and when the season kicked off in Melbourne, 15 JCB 531-70 telescopic handlers would be trackside. The machines were fitted with special jib attachments to aid the recovery of any crashed cars.

2020 Testing times

The dreadful events surrounding the onset of the COVID-19 global pandemic and the rapid rise in infection rates gave everyone cause for concern, and although industry and the economy suffered, the main aim was to look after the health of the population.

Like many others, JCB factories closed as a result of the outbreak, but in March work began to help address a national shortage of ventilators that were so urgently needed for the treatment of Coronavirus patients.

Following a direct appeal from the Prime Minister, Lord Bamford promised to help "in any way the company could" and immediately mobilised a research and engineering team to look at possible ways to assist – one of which was to make special steel housings for a new ventilator design.

In the end, the device, designed by Dyson, did not proceed due to a fortunately diminishing demand, but JCB stepped up in other areas by supplying front-line workers with essential PPE equipment and also launching an international aid initiative to provide food for those in desperate need as a result of the pandemic.

Over the following months, the company's catering staff both in Staffordshire and in India produced more than 200,000 meals for distribution in the areas around the JCB factories – an initiative that was the idea of Lady Bamford, who praised the "amazing job done" by JCB staff.

'When we were approached by the Prime Minister, we were determined, as a British company, to help in any way we could'

LORD BAMFORD

Above: the ventilator housings that were ready to be produced at the JCB factory.

Left: as part of the company's efforts to support communities during the pandemic, JCB-sponsored athletes Adam Burgess and Ben Williams lifted 22 tonnes – the same weight as an excavator – in three hours to raise more than £2,200 for the Royal Stoke Hospital. The pair will be representing Team GB at the 2021 Tokyo Olympics.

Left: JCB catering staff in India produced 175,000 meals to help local communities affected by the COVID-19 pandemic, while the UK prepared 35,000 meals and 8,000 sandwiches for the Staffordshire area suffering as a result of shortages and economic hardship.

Above: offering a glimmer of hope, the JCB Academy became one of the first schools in England to restart teaching after the pandemic dictated nationwide closures. The new Principal, Jenny McGuirk, explained how crucial it was to address the shortage of young people with engineering and business skills: "It's now time to get back to the business of teaching, to build on the success of the last decade, and to put the next generation of students on the road to success as we work with the challenges COVID-19 presents."

2020 BACKHOE RETURNED TO FORMER GLORY BY JCB

How do you say thank you to a loyal customer who has been buying your products since 1959? You restore the family digger, of course!

Lincolnshire firm Eric Carnaby & Son has bought more than 150 machines from JCB over the past six decades, and one that it has been meaning to restore for years is its cherished 1964 JCB 1 backhoe.

Running a business kept getting in the way, however, so when George Bamford surprised them with the news that the family firm was going to do it for them, Director Roland Carnaby Junior was over the moon.

Six months later, the completed machine was handed back after an extensive restoration and proudly wearing the Carnaby name. "It has been amazing to see an old machine brought back to life by the JCB team," exclaimed George Bamford. "It looks just as it would have done on the day it came off the production line in 1964."

DEVOTED TO THE CAUSE

Christopher McLaughlin is a true JCB 'superfan' – he even used to write to Anthony Bamford as a teenager, but now runs his own quarrying business and has expanded his fleet with the addition of a Hydradig 110W Wastemaster.

McLaughlin doesn't make any secret of his admiration for JCB and his office is a shrine to the company, its products and the people behind them. "I've been a JCB fan all my life – some people are fans of Manchester United, I'm a fan of JCB. I'm a JCB nerd and proud of it."

2020 750,000th BACKHOE

As JCB turned 75, another milestone was reached with the completion of the 750,000th backhoe loader. The special edition JCB 3CX, in its unique livery, may be in stark contrast to the 35 machines made in the first full year of production in 1954, but the inspiration and ethos behind it remains the same, as Lord Bamford recalled: "It really is testament to the versatility of the machine that its popularity continues to endure and will see it continue to prosper in the future."

Pictured are (left to right) Nihal Dhillon, Phil Starbuck – who retired in July 2020 and was the longest-serving employee in the backhoe loader business unit – John Plant, Lord Bamford, Shannon Ramczykowski and Keith Bloor.

THE CUSTOMER IS ALWAYS RIGHT

Founded in 1963, JC Balls & Sons is a plant hirer and contractor with a long-standing relationship with JCB, having first put its faith in one of the company's machines 57 years ago.

Director Jim Balls – 92 years old at the time of writing – bought a JCB 3 in 1963 and has been a customer since, testifying to the excellent levels of service and support his company has received. Proof of this is the fact that his company – which is now run by Jim's sons, Kevin and Christopher – has bought hundreds of JCB machines over the years, including one that Kevin believes to have been built by Mr JCB to tow his company jet.

However, the latest model to join the fleet is something very special: in October 2020, JC Balls & Sons bought the 750,000th backhoe!

Below: marking JCB's 75th birthday in appropriate style – a Fastrac ploughed the company's anniversary logo into a Staffordshire field in October 2020. The artwork was the size of four football pitches and could be seen by satellites orbiting the earth!

Above: with the completion of a brand-new £50 million plant in Uttoxeter, the company finalised the transfer of cab production from the old factory in Rugeley to the purpose-built facility. The new JCB Cab Systems factory is one of the most advanced in the world and features a computer-controlled production line, robotic welding and a fully automated painting facility.

Advertising & promotion

JCB has spent 75 years creating some of the most unique and striking pieces of promotional material within the industry. Here are just some of the best...

Some of the earliest advertisements majored on the strength of JCB's products – a theme that would consistently return over the next seven decades.

PUSH AHEAD
WITH YOUR JCB
HYDRA·DIGGA / LOADALL 65

MASSIVE and MIGHTY

The JCB HYDRA·DIGGA / LOADALL 65 is the most versatile, powerful and safest hydraulic earthmoving equipment available. The power and strength has been more than proved over the years, and is the ideal unit for the smallest builder and the largest contractor.

Early promotion followed the trend at the time for a combination of photography and illustration work, but the typography and messages were always simple, bold and very effective.

PROFILE Cedric Brookes

When Cedric Brookes began working with JCB in 1965, it was without doubt the start of an amazing adventure.

Brookes was the founder of an advertising company that had JCB as its major client and which would mastermind some of the most successful ad campaigns, but life working with JCB wasn't without its demands: "Only one thing mattered – to be the best. Weekends or nights – it mattered not, and if it needed to be done, it was done."

That ethos, shared with Joseph Bamford, resulted in a dedicated team that believed they could produce material that could see off the competition – even if it meant pushing themselves to the limit, as a loading shovel launch proved: "The main event was a theatre presentation including a new audio visual concept – rear projection. We devised an ambitious programme involving nine screens and 18 projectors, which resulted in three of us working the last few days and nights without returning home. We made it, but only by the skin of our teeth. After the show, Mr JCB came and sat alongside me and said, 'CAT couldn't have done that.' I knew then that we'd pulled it off."

One aspect that aided the creation of some truly unique advertising campaigns over the past 75 years was the positioning of JCB as a 'brand', as Brookes explains: "We believed that propositions are more important than justifications... benefits are more important than features. For example, one campaign had a simple strategy: to persuade our target audiences that they

could buy JCB with confidence because JCB would go to extraordinary lengths to look after them."

One of Brookes' most successful ads, however, was 'Buy British Beef' for the Fastrac campaign. "At the time, UK farmers were suffering because of 'mad cow' disease," he says, "but research showed that they believed that the ad demonstrated how JCB understood them. Some even displayed the ad in their tractors and it won many major advertising awards. A great company and great days."

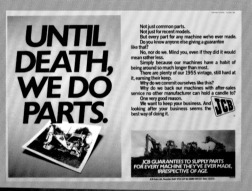

UNTIL DEATH, WE DO PARTS.

JCB GUARANTEES TO SUPPLY PARTS FOR EVERY MACHINE THEY'VE EVER MADE, IRRESPECTIVE OF AGE.

BUY BRITISH BEEF.

Top: one campaign that communicated just how well JCB would look after your purchase.
Above: 'Buy British Beef' was a hit with farmers.

CONTRACT JOURNAL 19th OCTOBER 1967

the
new
JCB
2B

2B

JCB

its been
well worth
waiting
for–

As the company moved into the 1960s, there was a shift into photography-based material. Finally the potential customer could see the striking core colours of the JCB range in some well-executed ads and brochures.

SPECIFY JCB FOR HIRE

JCB 3

SEE THE 3

THE COMPACT DIGGER WITH THE POWER-SLIDE KINGPOST

3 BY JCB

sleek styling
superb handling
3/4 cu. yd. bucket
this is the
fast super-powered **JCB** 7c
the machine
for the
really big jobs

THE UNBEATABLE **JCB** 4

WITH THE REVOLUTIONARY 3 IN I BUCKET

Big New Features to bring you extra profit!

★ Greater power from larger standardized rams and vane type pump.

★ Twin Ram "Smoothmatic" hydraulically cushioned rack and pinion slewing.

★ "Spaceview" super comfort cab can seat 5.

★ Standardized Hydraulics using 3 digger hoses only.

★ 30% increase in bucket capacities.

★ 3 in 1 multi purpose bucket—Face Shovel—Back Acter—Square Holes.

★ Full deluxe lighting for maximum machine usage.

★ Plus many other improvements and new features.

JCB Rocester, Staffs ☎ 432

clip off here

Mail this coupon NOW

for immediate information to

JCB Rocester, Staffs

Please rush details of the

NEW JCB 4

to..............................

C.J. 19·5

Industry journal adverts such as this one for the JCB 4 were often a little more straightforward in their approach, but their aim was simple: inform potential customers of the unique selling points and let them know how they can't possibly survive without adding one to the company fleet!

A PAIR OF SOCKS FOR CHRISTMAS.

(JUST WHAT YOU'VE ALWAYS WANTED).

£600 VOUCHER

REDEEMABLE AGAINST PURCHASE OF

ANY JCB LOADALL

£1,100 VOUCHER

REDEEMABLE AGAINST PURCHASE OF

THE JCB FARM SPECIAL

A PAIR OF SOCKS FOR CHRISTMAS.

(JUST WHAT YOU'VE ALWAYS WANTED).

Another innovative approach from the JCB advertising team – this time turning a pair of socks into an unmissable offer to round off 1983.

but only a JCB has them all!

Most excavators have some JCB features

JCB never shied away from involving the competition in its advertisements – particularly when it had some fact-based boasts to use as the core message, as with these two examples of 3C material.

Once we get our teeth in, we hold on!

Some British manufacturers have earned us all a bad reputation for poor after sales service, inadequate parts stocks, and ducking out of a market when it gets a little tight.

That's why in some export territories there is a resistance towards any British manufacturer. And this resistance has to be broken down.

At JCB we go to great lengths to show that we are here to stay. Like forming our own subsidiary companies to provide a dealer back-up on service and parts. Like sending out an Export Promotion Team to give sales and service training, to train demonstrators, to organise local advertising campaigns, etc.

The object is to convince the locals that we mean business. And we do.

J. C. Bamford Excavators Limited, Rocester, Uttoxeter, Staffordshire ST14 5JP

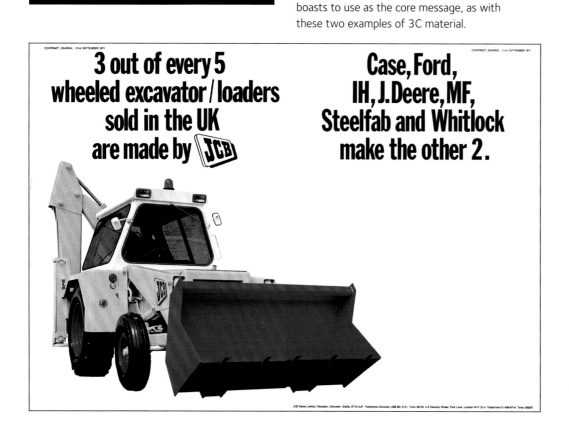

3 out of every 5 wheeled excavator/loaders sold in the UK are made by JCB

Case, Ford, IH, J.Deere, MF, Steelfab and Whitlock make the other 2.

Profit!

JCB 5C - increased profit for you

This **JCB** Mk1 cost builders T. & J. Brown less than 10/- a week to maintain over twelve years of hard work

In June 1955 Browns of Whaley Bridge bought their **JCB** Mk1 Since then, it has cost £300 to maintain, including tyres, parts, service etc. — approximately 2d per hour

In July 1967, T. & J. Brown bought their **JCB** 3C.

JCB Rocester, Uttoxeter, Staffs.

So.... they bought another **JCB**

"YOU ASKED FOR IT!"

See the new crawler mounted **JCB** 7, the machine you have all been waiting for—on Stand D15 at the Public Works Exhibition.

"I'll order twelve" says Roy Richards as he previews the new crawler mounted **JCB** 7 with Mr J. C. Bamford

Roy Richards - of Richards and Wallington - Britain's leading plant hire operator owns a fleet of 100 **JCB** excavators which he is still expanding.

Customer loyalty was frequently used to persuade others of JCB's dependability and worth – fortunately there was no shortage of testimonial messages on offer.

Citanduy, Indonesia. Humidity 82%. Temperature 33°C.

NO PLACE FOR SECOND BEST.

J. C. Bamford Excavators Limited, Rocester, Staffordshire, England ST14 5JP. Telephone: Rocester (0889) 590312. Telex: 36372.

A set of advertisements from the 1970s all used the same strapline but were shot in very different locations. From Indonesia to Western Australia, each demonstrated how JCB machines would still get the job done despite being put to work in some very demanding environments.

Kalgoorlie, Western Australia, temperature 46°C.

NO PLACE FOR SECOND BEST.

Refaa, Bahrain. Temperature 46°C.

NO PLACE FOR SECOND BEST.

JCB 3C
"A legend in its own time"
By JCB Circa 1973

How will the new JCB Farm Master compete with its nearest rival?

Gentle, sensitive, precise and sophisticated. That's *Vari-matic*.

To make a machine this advanced we left no stone unturned.

The new JCB 435.

"Nothing can beat it on top work."
J. Ponzo, Wiltshire.

More bold ads from the creative team. Strong copywriting, great photography and striking design made for decades of successful promotion.

GO FASTER STRIPES.

Out in the field where it matters most, nothing can touch (or catch) the remarkable JCB Fastrac. Its unique self-levelling hydro pneumatic suspension and equal weight distribution combine to minimise soil compaction. The suspen...

work, thus maximising pr...

how quickly the Fastrac c...

DRIVING IS BELIEVING.

YOU'RE LOOKING AT THE WORLD'S SAFEST SKID STEER.

In our view, no other skid steer has so many features contributing to operational safety. As you can clearly see.

IT PAYS TO SPECIFY JCB.

4 x 4 x 4 = JCB

JCB. THE FORMULA FOR THE 90's.

THINK BIG. THINK BIGGER.

THE JCB 801.   THE NEW JCB 803.

JCB. THE FORMULA FOR THE 90's.

A WHEELED EXCAVATOR WITH AN OUTSTANDING TRACK RECORD.

A JAPANESE EXCAVATOR THAT'S LOST NOTHING IN TRANSLATION.

The JCB backhoe loader cab.
Come in, sit down,
put your cubic feet up.

A Product of Hard Work

JCB Attachments. Completing the solution.

www.jcb.com

JCB models

They say that small is beautiful and an impressive number of scale JCB models have been made over the years, recreating some of the company's most iconic machines

SCALE MODELS FOR DEVELOPMENT WORK

JCB has for decades produced scale models as part of the development of a particular model. To begin with, these were made from lightweight materials such as plywood and aluminium, and some of the models are still on display within JCB HQ, but these days contemporary techniques have taken over and the models are built by 'rapid prototyping' the parts using the company's in-house 3D printers.

These are then handed over to professional model-makers and given specified paint finishes and decals. The models are usually 1:10 scale and are used to review concept directions before committing to full-scale prototypes.

From top: a limited-edition model produced by Border Fine Arts from 2002; a rare Tomica-Dandy JCB 3D; a super-detailed model of one of the company's earliest machines – now on display in The Story of JCB exhibition.

Top: Mr JCB and Anthony Bamford in 1978 with a scale model 3C Mk III. Above: the modern equivalent, produced with the aid of cutting-edge technology.

250g

Every JCB fan's dream
– to find a backhoe
loader in their cereal!

A new scale model of the 3C Mk III was produced by Britains in 2013 and was unveiled at JCB headquarters. Here it is in front of the real thing – a 3C recently restored by Julian Carder.

Right: a Corgi 1:50 model of the JCB 3C Mk I.

Below: two models produced by German modelmaker NZG – a 3C Mk III and a 3C Mk II, which is now highly sought after.

Above: the first scale model of a JCB – an Airfix kit of the JCB 3 backhoe loader, introduced in 1964. As with many collectable kits from that time, even the boxes were a work of art.

One of the biggest current producers of JCB scale models is Oxford Diecast. Its range of 1:76 machines includes a 75th anniversary pack, available in a special presentation box.

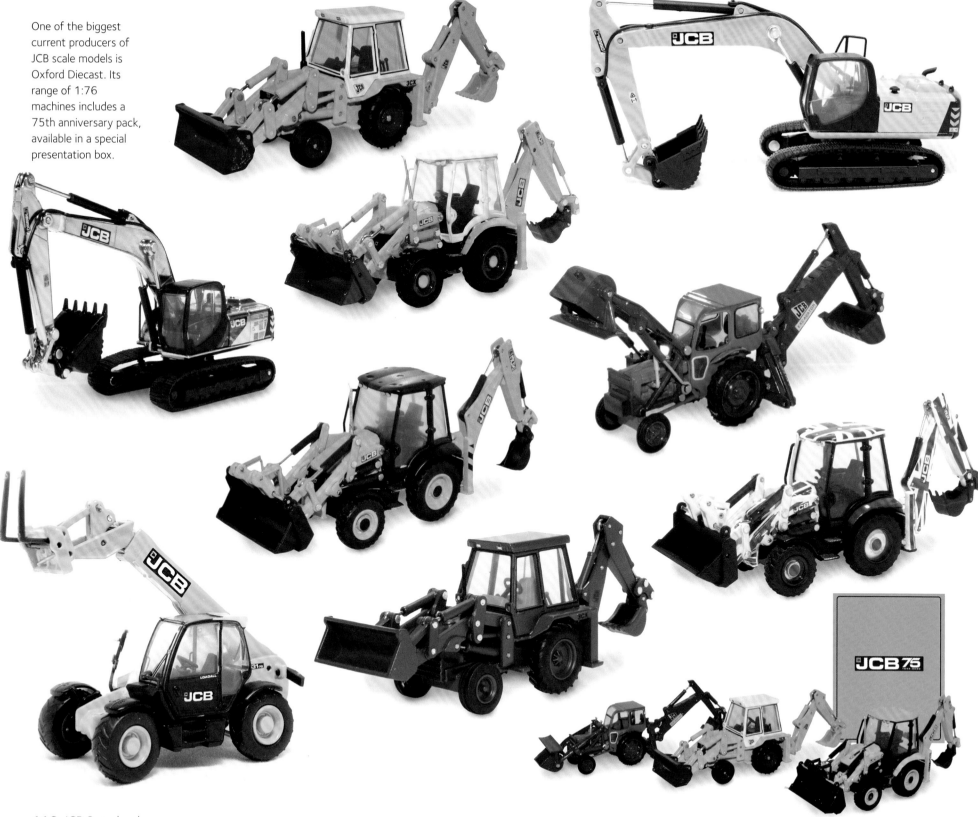

JCB MODELS
A COLLECTORS' GUIDE

There is certainly no shortage of JCB models on the market and these days you can buy everything from a Major Loader to a Fastrac, but without doubt the most popular machine among scale model collectors is the 3C range.

Early examples were produced by German company NZG and were well-made diecast models with a healthy amount of detail. With a number of variants produced, including a 3C Mk II with tinted glass for hot-climate export, some older models are highly collectable and command a price tag to match.

One definite rarity is a limited-edition gold 3C Mk II handed only to very important visitors or as a retirement gift to long-serving employees – as was a glass 'JCB in a bottle' by Lichfield Glass Sculpture, with one being presented to HRH The Prince of Wales in 1977.

Perhaps unsurprisingly, there is also a healthy market for model modification with skilful individuals producing bespoke adaptations to match period options. With many hours of work going into creating accurate representations, they certainly aren't cheap, but for the serious collector and JCB enthusiast it's a price worth paying.

Another offering from Oxford Diecast: the de Havilland Dove – JCB's first plane.

For many years Britains has produced family-favourite farm toys and its range now includes several offerings from the JCB stable. Among them are the 3CX backhoe loaders (below) and 25th anniversary Fastrac model (bottom right), which is limited to just 5,000 units.

JCB record breakers

Think of earth-moving machinery and the first thing that springs to mind isn't necessarily a thirst for speed, but you might be surprised to discover that JCB has a penchant for performance...

Did you know?

The Dieselmax was pushed from behind by a JCB Fastrac until it reached 30mph. At this point, the streamliner could engage first gear!

JCB DIESELMAX

WHEN? 23 AUGUST 2006

WHERE? BONNEVILLE, USA

HOW FAST? 350.092MPH

The origins of JCB's land speed record stem directly from Lord Bamford's school years, when he read about tales of daring and high-speed adventure in *The Eagle* and *Boy's Own*; Malcolm Campbell and Stirling Moss were just two of the names that would subsequently come to inspire the company's attempt in 2006.

The initial idea soon began to take shape and it was decided that the vehicle would be powered by a pair of JCB's own 444 diesel engines, but the team also brought former land speed record holder Richard Noble on board. Noble assisted in many aspects of the project, including a crucial question: who would be 'at the wheel'?

Noble had little doubt and the question was put to Wing Commander Andy Green – a former fighter pilot and land speed record holder with ThrustSSC, achieving a figure of 763.035mph in 1997. Green immediately said yes to JCB's proposal and the attempt had a driver.

Remarkably, it took just 18 months to develop the vehicle and in July 2006 the JCB Dieselmax was ready for its first test runs at RAF Wittering near Peterborough – just three weeks before Bonneville Speed Week was due to begin and their attempt slot presented itself.

Testing was not without issue, but the team pulled together and the Salt Flats now lay ahead. On 17 August, the various 'qualifying' runs began. Once again, these were not plain sailing and once again, the dedicated team who had lived and breathed the Dieselmax project for so long pulled out all the stops. On 23 August, Green set out on what would be the pivotal run.

Having already clocked up 328mph the day before – a diesel-powered record – the team decided to aim for the 350 mark, and at 7:37am the vehicle began its first attempt, clocking an amazing 365.74mph. The second run suffered from a slow start and was recorded at 335.695mph, but after a nervous wait, the result came over the radio: average speed, 350.092mph. JCB was officially a record holder.

Wing Commander Andy Green may have been at the controls for the diesel-engined land speed record attempt, but it was the dedication and ingenuity of the entire JCB team that achieved the remarkable result.

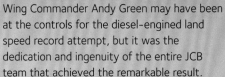

JCB444-LSR

THE ENGINE BEHIND THE RECORD ATTEMPT

It started out as a modest 140bhp engine designed to go into a digger, but by the time it reached the Dieselmax record-attempt car, it had been developed into a 750bhp powerhouse!

Having been bored out to five litres, two-stage turbocharging was added and an all-new fuel system developed specifically for the attempt.

The final arrangement featured two JCB444-LSR engines – one driving the front and one powering the rear wheels.

Did you know?

Fastrac Two could, in theory, run on vegetable oil, but for the record attempt the team used high-performance racing diesel and achieved just over 5mpg!

WORLD'S FASTEST TRACTOR

WHEN? 23 OCTOBER 2019

WHERE? ELVINGTON, UK

HOW FAST? 135.191MPH

It takes a special kind of outfit to set a record and then embark on a mission to top its own figure just months later, but that's exactly what JCB did in 2019. With the first incarnation of its high-speed tractor – a modified version of Fastrac – JCB set a record of 103.6mph in June, but come November it was back at Elvington Airfield in Yorkshire to try to better that record.

Motorcycle racer and lorry mechanic Guy Martin was again at the wheel, but the new and improved tractor – Fastrac Two – boasted some impressive tweaks over its predecessor. For starters, the package was 10% lighter and, thanks to new streamlined bodywork and aerodynamic development, also boasted a 10% reduction in drag.

The tractor was powered by a 7.2-litre six-cylinder JCB 672 Dieselmax engine with the addition of an electrically driven supercharger and a larger turbocharger than previously, boosted by water injection and charge-air cooling through ice tanks – reducing intake temperatures by 50°C. All of that development resulted in a peak

power output of 1,016hp at 3,150rpm, with over 2,500Nm of torque!

Perhaps the biggest challenge, however, was that of the tyres, which were 1.3m tall, weighed 80kg and were usually rated for 40mph. JCB set about developing a new product for the job and created a tyre approved for speeds up to 161mph.

On the day of the record run, Guy Martin took Fastrac Two to a peak speed of 153.771mph. The average speed, and the one recorded and verified by Guinness World Records, eventually came out as being 135.191mph – smashing its previous record by more than 30mph!

When JCB originally developed its Fastrac tractor in 1991, setting speed records was not the motivation, but the company since proved it was a force to be reckoned with... twice!

FASTEST TRACTOR DRIVER IN THE WEST
GUY MARTIN

So what exactly was it like to drive the fastest tractor in the world? Guy Martin offers an insight...

"Well, it can't turn very tightly because it doesn't have a rear differential," he explains. "You also need to get used to how the gears change. It's fairly sluggish until the turbo kicks in, but it doesn't feel that fast – Elvington Airfield is a big open place and you don't have anything to reference your speed against."

According to Martin, it doesn't feel like a tractor, either: "From the outside it may look like a tractor, but it doesn't to sit in and it certainly doesn't go like one. You have a five-point harness, there's no radio, no cup holder, no fridge – most tractors have a fridge and air-conditioning!"

Fortunately though, the lack of home comforts didn't stop Martin from having some faith in what the team could achieve: "I knew for ages that we could do it. There were some clever people involved and I knew that when they said they were going to break the record, it was going to happen. I had no doubt."

1970 WORLD CUP RALLY

WHEN? APRIL–MAY 1970

WHERE? LONDON–MEXICO

HOW FAR? 16,000 MILES

JCB's passion for going fast on four wheels began long before any record attempts, and in 1970 it added its backing, name and colour to an entry into the 1970 World Cup Rally.

The JCB-yellow and red Hillman Hunter GT set off along with 95 other vehicles from Wembley Stadium, bound for Mexico in an arduous and demanding endurance race that would last five weeks and cover 16,000 miles.

The crew, consisting of Peter Brown, British Rally champion John Bloxham and Ulster Rally champion Robert McBurney, would each take their turn at the wheel of the Hillman, driving against the clock to cover a variety of stages through an impressive number of countries – flying the flag for JCB as they went. In suitable World Cup style, Sir Alf Ramsey – England manager at the time – flagged the cars on their way.

Out of those 96 entries, only 26 completed the rally and unfortunately number 17, JCB 582, was not one of them, instead making up one of the 70 retirees.

Did you know?

As well as star drivers such as Rauno Aaltonen and Paddy Hopkirk, the rally included footballer Jimmy Greaves and HRH Prince Michael of Kent.

Clockwise from right: JCB 582 makes a splash on a pre-rally publicity trip; the Hillman in full trim being flagged off at Wembley; the team spent time training with Stoke City FC in a bid to make sure they were fit for the job; Anthony Bamford helps to check over the forthcoming route and discusses tactics with Brown and Bloxham!

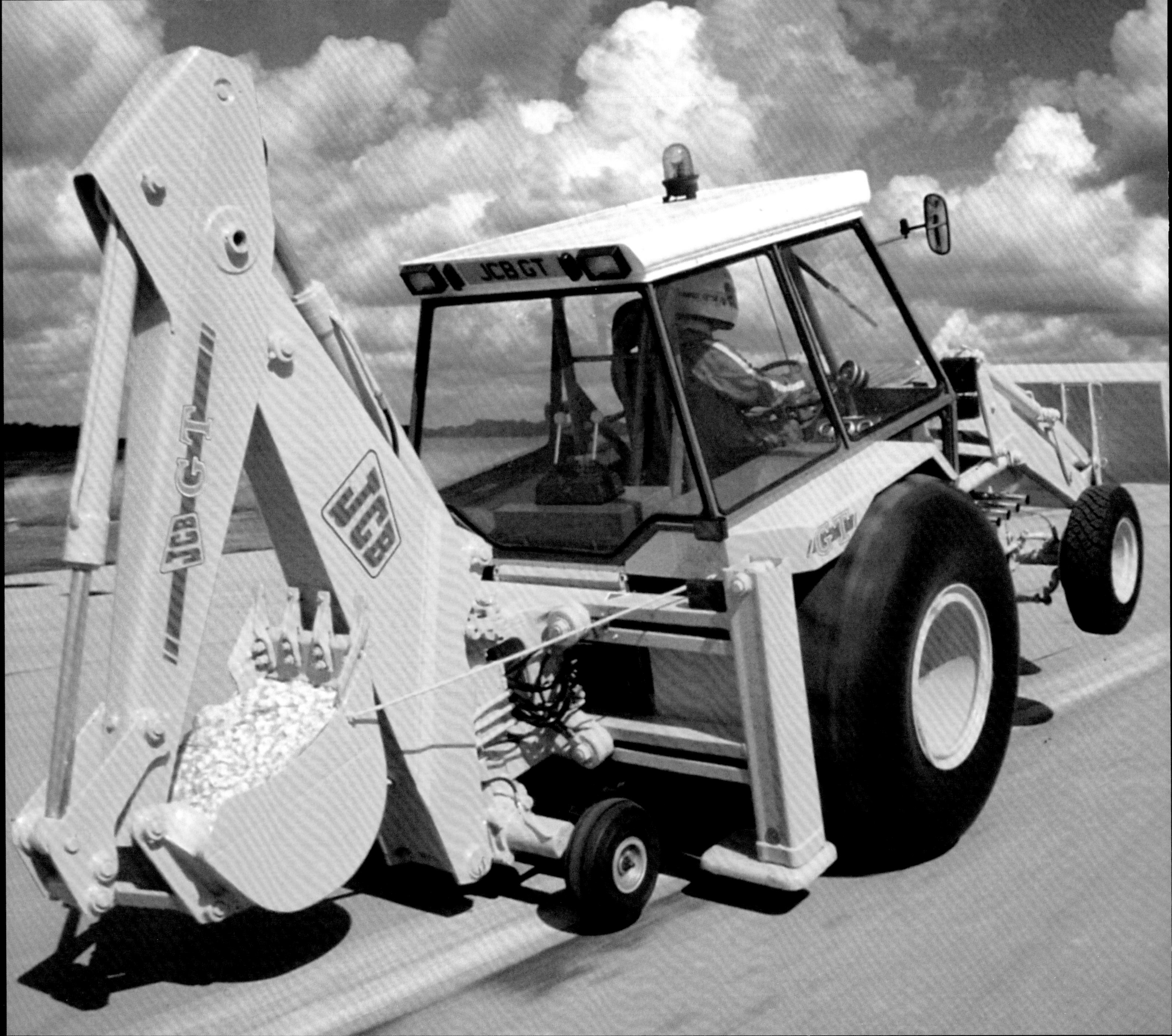
JCB GT
JCB GT
JCB
GT

JCB GT

WHEN?	1988/2014
WHERE?	UK & AUSTRALIA
HOW FAST?	72.58MPH

Some 31 years before Fastrac Two set a world record, JCB came up with the idea for a V8-powered backhoe loader. Although it took more than two years of research and development, the finished backhoe certainly packed a punch.

With a supercharged Chevrolet 'big block' engine and twin four-barrelled Holley carburettors, the supercharged V8 generated 1,000bhp when run on four-star fuel and was capable of pulling a wheelie as it accelerated down the track at Donington Park in August 1988.

At the wheel was Malcolm Grindey, JCB demonstrator and senior mechanic, who claimed at the time that it was "a real beast and totally different from anything I've ever driven." There was one issue with the wheelie-pulling GT, however: how to steer with the front wheels off the ground. This was eventually solved by fitting a pair of 'fiddle brakes' under the steering wheel that allowed for individual braking of the rear wheels, thus directing the speedy backhoe.

The GT's masterstroke, of course, was that it looked very much like a normal backhoe at first glance, although a closer look would reveal a steel spaceframe chassis clad with moulded glassfibre body and Perspex side windows – all of which helped keep the weight down.

Did you know?

The first JCB GT included a pair of jockey wheels taken from a Cessna aeroplane, running on modified trailer suspension to allow it to wheelie at a 23-degree angle.

The original JCB GT made appearances at events all over the world, including at the Formula One Australian Grand Prix in 1990. The GT was powered by a Chevy 'big block' V8 and became as famous for the noise it made as for its speed!

JCB GT
RECORD ATTEMPT, BATHURST, AUSTRALIA

Twenty-six years after the original JCB GT, the world would witness an updated version set a new record at Bathurst, Australia. With JCB demonstration driver Matthew Lucas at the wheel, the supercharged 572 'big block', now packing 1,300bhp, propelled the backhoe loader to a remarkable 72.58mph.

The JCB GT covered the quarter-mile in an impressive 17 seconds – impressive for a digger, that is, but features such as a loader and digger end made completely from aluminium, as well as a Fastrac rear axle, helped contribute to the weight savings and therefore its top speed.

Just several of the aircraft that have been operated by JCB since 1960, including its first, the de Havilland Dove (left), and the Hawker Siddeley HS 125 (main). The company duly announced the Dove purchase with pride, having placed the order in late 1960.

JCB TAKES TO THE SKIES

WHEN? 1960 ONWARDS

WHERE? 21,000FT+

HOW FAST? 200MPH+

Joseph Bamford knew from the start just how important it was to be able to travel overseas in order to explore new business markets and meet new customers. Similarly, he recognised the potential benefit of being able to bring those customers to the factory so that they could look at the company's latest product range. In 1960, JCB therefore bought its first aircraft – a twin-engined de Havilland Dove.

With that first plane came the formation of JCB Aviation and the company's first pilot, Captain Mike Sutton, but that initial venture set in motion a continued investment in air travel.

In 1970, JCB purchased its first Hawker Siddeley HS 125 Executive jet. With a cruising speed of 522mph, it was a significant improvement over the Dove, although thanks to the yellow-and-red colour scheme, it earned the nickname 'the bleeding banana'!

Since the Dove, JCB has operated more than a dozen planes and helicopters, and for many years the Rocester HQ has had a helipad on site.

Did you know?

Joseph Bamford was awarded his Aviator's Certificate by the Royal Aero Club of the United Kingdom in June 1948.

A global reach

It may have spent 75 years flying the flag for Great Britain, but JCB has done it in spectacular global fashion with an unequalled outlook on the worldwide construction industry

AROUND THE WORLD

Although JCB is a British company and extremely proud to be so, it has never even considered restricting its growth and appeal to the shores of the United Kingdom. From the very beginning, it has considered its market appeal to encompass all four corners of the earth.

Established in a rented lockup in Uttoxeter, JCB now has plants in 22 locations around the world, and its passion for exportation has resulted in its products being captured at work in some extremely impressive scenery…

Rock and a hard place: with temperatures pushing 40°C in the summer, you probably wouldn't want to be in the cab of your 3C II for long, but the juxtaposition of backhoe and the rock formations of Monument Valley, Colorado make for an impressive image.

JCB's headquarters at Rocester remain the hub for the company's operations despite a worldwide presence.

Joseph Bamford acknowledged just how crucial the global market could be to JCB's success. He was quick to recognise the efforts of employees in helping to secure overseas business, as demonstrated here by the efforts of Alan Cooper and Bob Nixon, who secured a very respectable order from Japan in the 1960s.

A JCB 3D II soaks up the sun as it goes to work in Toledo, Spain.

If there's one thing New Zealand is famous for, it's lamb. As this tracked loader is transported to site, it has to pause to make way for a local herd.

Clockwise from left: an articulated wheeled loader enters the picturesque streets of Biel, Switzerland; old meets new – a JCB 3D prepares to break ground with Rome's Colosseum as a backdrop; underneath the arches – JCB France delivers a new 3C II, pausing beneath the Eiffel Tower; flying the flag for JCB in Urbach on the outskirts of Cologne.

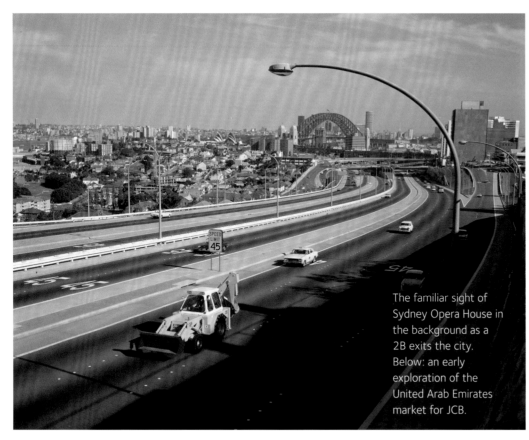

The familiar sight of Sydney Opera House in the background as a 2B exits the city. Below: an early exploration of the United Arab Emirates market for JCB.

GLOBAL STATISTICS

Although it started with just one person, JCB now employs more than 12,000 worldwide

There are over 750 JCB dealers currently in place around the world

JCB machines are now manufactured on four continents

JCB has 22 factories spread across the UK, India, USA, Brazil and China

According to latest figures, one in two of all construction industry machines sold in India are JCBs

JCB is the largest manufacturer of construction equipment in all of Europe

The company has 30 Queen's Awards for Technology and Export achievements

In 2010, a JCB 3CX drove from the east coast of the USA to the west, covering 3,184 miles in 26 days

A JCB 3C II on road-building duties in La Paz, Bolivia in 1972.

Did you know?

In 2007, JCB launched LiveLink, a telematics system that could monitor machines and assist with remote diagnostics – wherever you were in the world!

Clockwise from main: a 526 Loadall at work in Cambodia; JCB's factory in São Paulo, Brazil; Lord Bamford officially opening JCB India Limited in 2003; the impressive facility in Jaipur in 2014.

Top: a JCB 35D Teletruk was one of several sent out to help with the building of a football stadium in Johannesburg in preparation for the 2010 FIFA World Cup. Above: a JS200 contributes to a flood-defence project in Belo Horizonte, Brazil.

Right: JCB machines are regularly sent to help with rescue and clean-up efforts in the wake of natural disasters around the world, such as earthquakes and flooding.

Consumer Products

With a name that's renowned for performance, it's little wonder that JCB chose to apply it to a carefully considered range of products so that contractors and enthusiasts alike could indulge their love of the brand

POWER TOOLS

For a number of years now, the JCB name and the familiar yellow-and-black colour scheme have appeared on an impressive range of power tools and accessories.

From cordless drills to air compressors, all of them benefit from the company's stringent quality controls, and with an accessory range that also provides everything from sandpaper sheets and drill bits to hole saws and head lights, a comprehensive backup service is required in order to provide the necessary support for industry professionals and DiY enthusiasts.

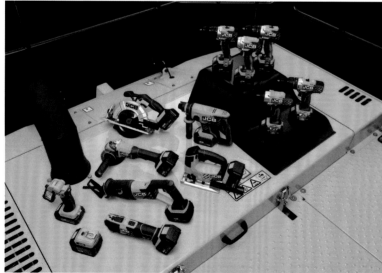

Above: farmer and *Countryfile* presenter Adam Henson shows off the range of JCB power tools and accessories.

From safety boots to spectacles, the JCB name now appears on a diverse selection of products, which even includes mobile phones that have been specifically designed to withstand the demands of life on site.

JCB FOR KIDS – STARTING THEM YOUNG!

Okay, so you may not end up with a Fastrac on the driveway for them to wash, as pictured here, but you can still kit out the kids in mini JCB overalls so they look the part. They can even have their own tools, and when the weather takes a turn for the worse they can disappear indoors and play with scale models of JCB's range of machinery. For the ultimate experience, though, they can get their hands on the controls of a mini digger at Gulliver's Kingdom Resort in Derbyshire!

The company has lent its support to this attraction in Derbyshire so that younger members of the family can really get the full JCB experience. These are the backhoe operators of the future...

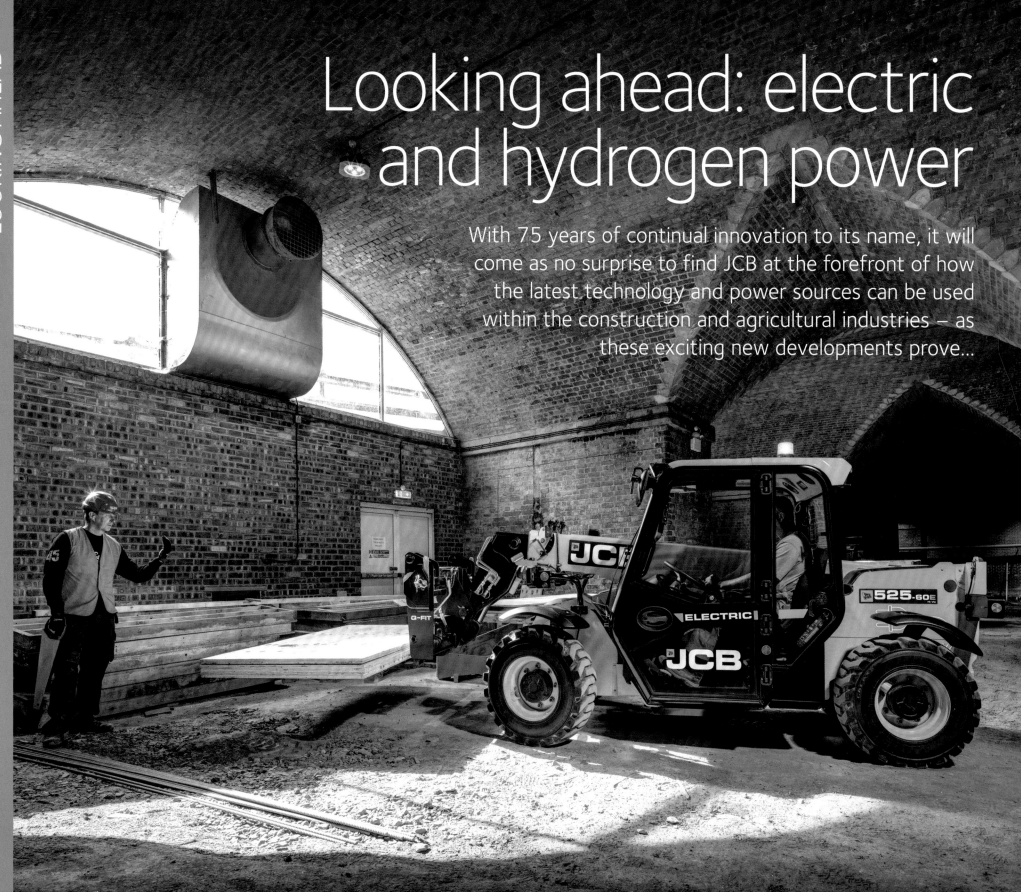

Looking ahead: electric and hydrogen power

With 75 years of continual innovation to its name, it will come as no surprise to find JCB at the forefront of how the latest technology and power sources can be used within the construction and agricultural industries – as these exciting new developments prove...

2020 ELECTRIC POWER

Following the highly successful launch of JCB's first electric-powered mini excavator in 2018, the company announced the expansion of its E-TECH range in the latter part of 2020.

More than 43 years after JCB developed the pioneering concept of the telescopic handler, the 525-60E – a fully electric-powered version – was unveiled, providing zero-emissions output yet designed to offer the same performance as its conventional diesel counterpart.

The new model relies on two electric motors: one to power the driveline and the second for the hydraulic system – both being 85% efficient compared to the 45% efficiency of a traditional diesel engine!

Further boosting the range will be JCB's first ever electric site dumper – the 1T-E. Featuring a full steel skip and heavy-duty articulated chassis, and with low noise levels, it's ideal for use on indoor, underground and emissions-sensitive sites.

Also in 2020, the 19C-1E electric excavator scooped a top award from the Royal Academy of Engineering, fighting off competition to pick up the MacRobert Award in recognition of manufacturing the world's first volume-produced fully electric digger.

Just some of JCB's latest E-TECH range of electrically powered machines. All boast zero emissions and the ability to operate at a much quieter level, making them ideal for use in noise-sensitive environments.

2020 HYDROGEN POWER

JCB's 75th anniversary year saw the innovation continue with the development of a prototype of the construction industry's first hydrogen-powered excavator – leading the sector on zero and low carbon emission technology.

With more than 12 months of rigorous testing carried out at JCB's quarry proving grounds, the 220X excavator, powered by a hydrogen fuel cell, is a fully operational prototype and one that draws upon the experience of Lord Bamford's son Jo, who spent 14 years at JCB before setting up Ryse Hydrogen.

Power for the prototype excavator is generated by mixing hydrogen with oxygen in a fuel cell, creating energy to run electric motors. It's a very clean process – the only emission from the exhaust is water.

Following on from the company's first fully electric mini excavator and its innovations in clean diesel technology, the hydrogen-powered excavator is further proof of JCB's commitment to a cleaner construction industry for the future, as Lord Bamford was keen to emphasise: "JCB will continue to develop and refine this technology with advanced testing of our prototype hydrogen machine. We will continue to be at the forefront of technologies designed to build a zero carbon future."

Lord Bamford and son Jo with the hydrogen-powered 220X. Thanks to the reactive process inside the fuel cell, the only emission is water. Thus begins another innovative chapter in the story of JCB.